THE HISTORIC TRIANGLE

WILLIAMSBURG

JAMESTOWN & YORKTOWN

FODOR'S TRAVEL PUBLICATIONS

are compiled, researched, and edited by an international team of travel writers, field correspondents, and editors. The series, which now almost covers the globe, was founded by Eugene Fodor in 1936.

OFFICES
New York & London

Fodor's Williamsburg, Jamestown & Yorktown:

Editor: Richard T. Scott
Area Coordinator: Editorial Ink, Ltd.
Contributing Editors: E. K. Holmes, Eleanor H. Louttit, James Louttit, Russell Scurfield
Research: Grace Coughlan, Jacqueline Russell
Maps and Plans: Jon Bauch Design, Oliver Williams
Drawings: Amy Harold

WILLIAMSBURG

JAMESTOWN & YORKTOWN

FODOR'S TRAVEL PUBLICATIONS, INC.
New York & London

First Edition

The following Fodor's guides are currently available; most are also published in a British edition by Hodder & Stoughton.

Country and Area Guides

Australia, New Zealand
& the South Pacific
Austria
Bahamas
Belgium & Luxembourg
Bermuda
Brazil
Canada
Canada's Maritime
  Provinces
Caribbean
Central America
Eastern Europe
Egypt
Europe
France
Germany
Great Britain
Greece
Holland
Hungary
India, Nepal & Sri Lanka
Ireland
Israel
Italy
Japan
Jordan & the Holy Land
Kenya
Korea
Loire Valley
Mexico
New Zealand
North Africa
People's Republic
  of China
Portugal
Province of Quebec
Scandinavia
Scotland
South America
South Pacific
Southeast Asia
Soviet Union
Spain
Sweden
Switzerland
Turkey
Yugoslavia

City Guides

Amsterdam
Beijing, Guangzhou,
  Shanghai
Boston
Chicago
Dallas & Fort Worth
Florence & Venice
Greater Miami & the
  Gold Coast
Hong Kong
Houston & Galveston
Lisbon
London
Los Angeles
Madrid
Mexico City &
  Acapulco
Munich
New Orleans
New York City
Paris
Philadelphia
Rome
San Diego
San Francisco
Singapore
Stockholm, Copenhagen,
  Oslo, Helsinki &
  Reykjavik
Sydney
Tokyo
Toronto
Vienna
Washington, D.C.

U.S.A. Guides

Alaska
Arizona
Atlantic City & the
  New Jersey Shore
California
Cape Cod
Chesapeake
Colorado
Far West
Florida
Hawaii
I-10: California to Florida
I-55: Chicago to
  New Orleans
I-75: Michigan to Florida
I-80: San Francisco to
  New York
I-95: Maine to Miami

New England
New Mexico
New York State
Pacific North Coast
South
Texas
U.S.A.
Virginia
Williamsburg, Jamestown
  & Yorktown

Budget Travel

American Cities (30)
Britain
Canada
Caribbean
Europe
France
Germany
Hawaii
Italy
Japan
London
Mexico
Spain

Fun Guides

Acapulco
Bahamas
Las Vegas
London
Maui
Montreal
New Orleans
New York City
The Orlando Area
Paris
Puerto Rico
Rio
Riviera
St. Martin/Sint Maarten
San Francisco
Waikiki

Special-Interest Guides

The Bed & Breakfast Guide
Selected Hotels of Europe
Ski Resorts of North
  America
Views to Dine by around
  the World

CONTENTS

FACTS AT YOUR FINGERTIPS

THE STORY AND THE EXPERIENCE

PRACTICAL INFORMATION

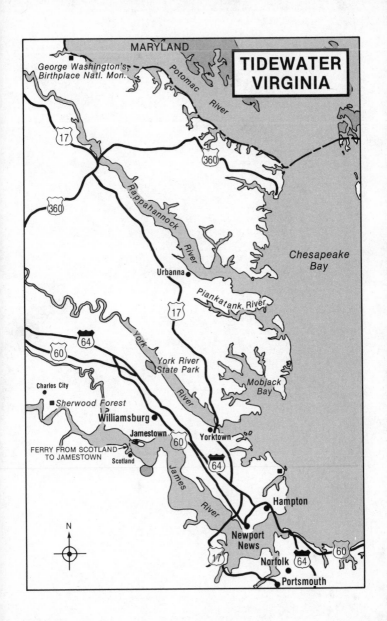

FOREWORD

A very dear friend, an Englishman and frequent visitor to the United States, recently informed us, with pitying undertones, "You people have no history." For a minute we were tempted to agree. Compared to the length and scope of British history, we were, figuratively speaking, "born yesterday." We *are* a British offspring, but in 1607 we left home to seek our fortune, and in 1776 we set up our own household.

All this is to introduce you to the first of Fodor's planned new series, the **Heritage Guides.** *Fodor's Williamsburg, Jamestown, and Yorktown* is a carefully researched guide to the life and times of those generations of Anglo-Americans who cut the apron strings of their mother country and came of age in a new land. The format is slightly different from other Fodor's guides. As usual we have attempted to offer you a comprehensive listing of lodgings and restaurants as well as things to see and do, but in addition we have tried to give you a glimpse of what those first years of America were really like.

"Facts at Your Fingertips," the first section of *Fodor's Williamsburg, Jamestown, and Yorktown,* is designed to help you plan your trip, providing general information on activities and attractions as well as local facts on climate, transportation, and the like.

Next is "The Story," an account of what happened, when it happened, and where it happened. We have omitted most of the "why" it happened, since ours is a story, not a history lesson. While a list of "who" it happened to would probably fill an entire book itself, we hope that our guide will, vicariously, make you one of them.

"The Experience" is a description of how to explore this triangle of history located on the Virginia Peninsula. Here we have attempted to give you an orderly sequential, chronologically correct tour of the three sites. The "Practical Information" section includes descriptions, addresses, phone numbers, and other particulars on accommodations, restaurants, museums, and more.

You should know that the selections and comments in *Fodor's Williamsburg, Jamestown, and Yorktown* are based on personal experience and be aware that all data is accurate as we go to press but that later changes can and most likely will occur. We sincerely welcome your letters about these changes and will revise our entries for future editions when the facts warrant it.

Send your letter to the Publisher at Fodor's Travel Publications, 201 East 50th Street, New York, NY 10022. Continental or British Commonwealth readers may prefer to write Fodor's Travel Publications, 9–10 Market Place, London W1N 7AG, England.

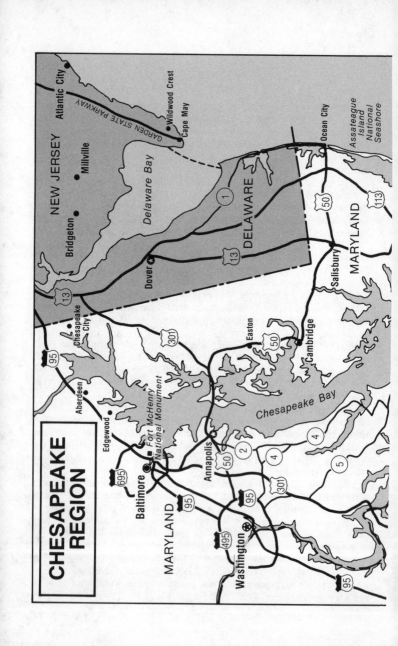

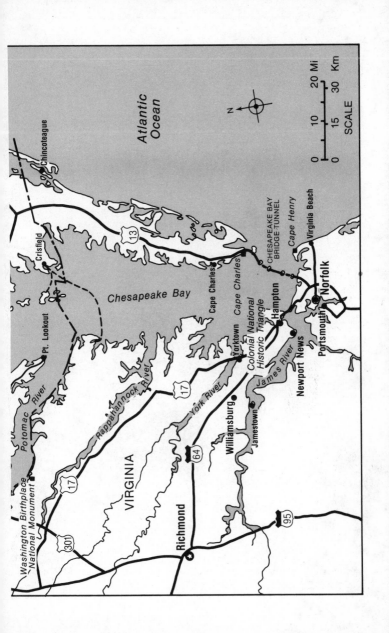

PREFACE

Getting the Most Out of the Historic Triangle

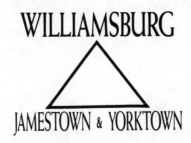

WILLIAMSBURG

JAMESTOWN & YORKTOWN

Colonial Williamsburg is the star, and for that it deserves our thanks and applause.

But Williamsburg is only part of the story; it is the second part, the *middle* part — Act II in a three-act play.

If Williamsburg is a smash Act II (and it is), Jamestown sets the scene in a hopeful but traumatic Act I, while Yorktown rings down the curtain with a thundering and moving Act III.

Years of preparation, millions of dollars, and the efforts of thousands of planners, builders, artisans, and craftsmen have gone into making Colonial Williamsburg, Jamestown, and Yorktown a traveler's treat. To praise any one of the three in no way diminishes the others; but to overlook any one would be a serious omission.

Any really good story (and the Historic Triangle is one of the best) should be enjoyed in its proper sequence — from the beginning, through the middle, to the end. We believe that *this* story is no exception and should also be experienced in sequence, though it grew out of earlier visits to the three villages, when we mistakenly toured and explored helter-skelter. During subsequent visits we observed others making those same mistakes.

This Heritage Series guidebook, therefore, follows the natural order of events — beginning on the marshy lowlands along the James, moving inland to a new and vigorous Colonial town, and concluding in the fields south of Yorktown. The book follows this sequence in both the opening narrative chapters, "the Story" and "the Experience," and in its later Practical Information chapters — Places to Stay, Places to Eat, and Things to See and Do.

The Historic Triangle covers a relatively small area (note map on following pages) and it is possible to tour each of these three villages during even the shortest of visits.

Familiarize yourself with this guide before you begin, then give each site the time you feel it deserves.

If you truly want to get the most out of this touring experience, follow our advice and tour them in sequence; don't deprive yourself of the full impact of these three historic gems.

—the Editors

MAP OF THE
HISTORIC TRIANGLE

WILLIAMSBURG

JAMESTOWN & YORKTOWN

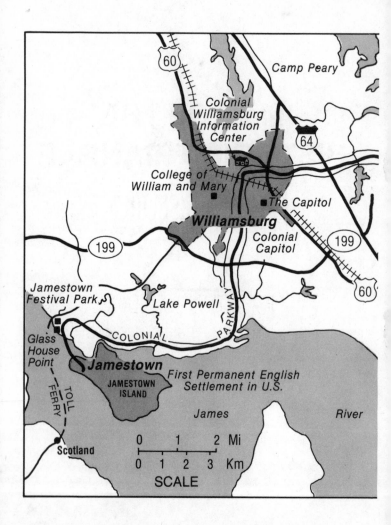

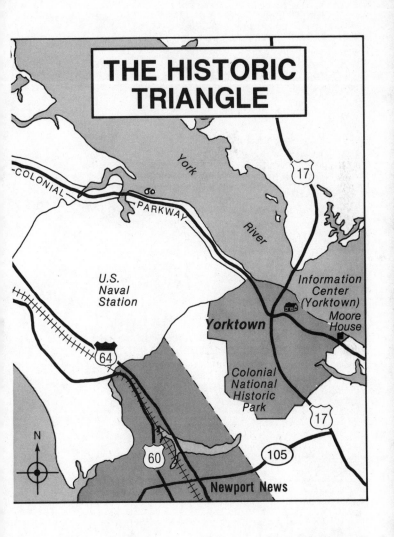

FACTS AT YOUR FINGERTIPS

WHAT IT IS. Geographically, the historic trio of Jamestown, Williamsburg, and Yorktown shares a relatively small stage — a wooded triangle on the Virginia Peninsula that measures little more than a dozen miles between its most distant points. Historically, these three Colonial period gems have held center stage for 175 years (1607–1781), yet spanned three fascinating "acts," the beginning, middle, and end of America's turbulent Colonial experience. Emotionally, the Jamestown-Williamsburg-Yorktown story today is a moving and inspiring touring experience.

WHERE IT IS. The Historic Triangle is located near the midpoint on Virginia's southernmost peninsula, just above the Norfolk, Newport News, and Hampton complex, about 40 miles southeast of Richmond.

Jamestown, Williamsburg, and Yorktown form an obtuse triangle that encompasses an area of slightly more than 30 square miles. The triangle measures about six straight-line miles along one side, 11 on another, and a little less than 15 across its Jamestown-Yorktown base.

The Virginia Peninsula itself fronts the York River to the north and the James River to the south, while its southeastern tip dips into Hampton Roads and lower Chesapeake Bay. This is one of the four Tidewater peninsulas of Virginia. (Three, including this peninsula, are on the Chesapeake's western shore; the fourth, to the east, fronts the Atlantic.) The name "Tidewater" conjures up a vision of the area — a sandy, gentle low-lying land, moist with sea air, and drained by wide, slow rivers. Located in America's mid-Atlantic region (just above 37° N. Lat. and slightly east of 77° W. Long.), the peninsula is a lush and pleasant land, often washed and freshly laundered by its abundance of water and sunshine, but also occasionally parboiled by a steamy combination of the two.

HOW TO GET THERE. The Historic Triangle is twice blessed by its Tidewater Virginia location: first, for its temperate Southern climate, and second, but no less important, for its accessibility. Although much of each of the three sites can and should be explored on foot, some form of wheeled transportation is necessary for getting from one to another. Here is how to reach the general area:

By Car. The Virginia Peninsula is bisected along its length (NW–SE) by I–64 and U.S. 60 (Richmond Road), west toward Richmond, east toward Norfolk. Rte. 5 winds along the James River between Richmond and Williamsburg, while U.S. 17 enters the peninsula at Yorktown, spanning the York River from Gloucester Point to the north. Williamsburg, at the heart of the Triangle, can be reached from I–64, Exit 56 (Rte. 132, closer to Richmond) or Exit 57 (Rte. 199, closer to Norfolk). The scenic Colonial Parkway curves through and sometimes *under* Colonial Williamsburg, linking Jamestown to the southwest, with Yorktown to the southeast. Also noteworthy are Jamestown Road (Rte. 31), between Jamestown and Williamsburg; the U.S. 60 Bypass Road, just north of Colonial Williamsburg; and Merrimac Trail (Rte. 143), east of Williamsburg and south toward Newport News. The Historic Triangle is 40 miles southeast of Richmond, 40 miles northwest of Norfolk, 150 miles south of Washington, D.C. (via I–95 and I–64), 380 miles south of New York City, and 185 miles northeast of Raleigh-Durham, N.C.

By Air. Patrick Henry International Airport, on the Peninsula between Williamsburg and Hampton Roads, is 20 minutes from Colonial Williamsburg; Byrd International Airport in Richmond and Norfolk International Airport are each approximately an hour's drive away. All three airports are served by a number of major airlines, and ground transportation is available for all flights. The smaller general-aviation Jamestown-Williamsburg Airport is three miles south of downtown Williamsburg, off Rte. 199.

By Bus. Nationwide service by Greyhound; Trailways serves Richmond and Norfolk, with connections to Williamsburg.

By Train. Direct *Amtrak* service from Boston, New York, Philadelphia, Baltimore, Washington, and Richmond.

WHEN TO GO. The climate in the Historic Triangle is relatively mild throughout the year. While the high humidity in summer does make the 80°F average daily temperature seem higher, it is often offset by breezes from the water nearby. There is some snow in winter, most often during January and February, but the average daily temperature is still 45°F. Spring and fall are especially pleasant times to visit, if you don't mind taking along a sweater or light jacket for the cool evenings. The crowds are thinner before May and after September, and are pleasantly sparse during mid-winter months. If you're not dependent on work- or school–vacation schedules, or especially if you're visiting for the feel of the area's history, try to make your trip off-season to take advantage of the reduced rates often offered.

Average Temperature and Rainfall

Spring

March, 48°F; April, 57°F; May, 67°F . . . 10.18 inches

Summer

June, 75°F; July, 78°F; August, 79°F . . . 14.21 inches

Fall

September, 71°F; October, 61°F; November, 50°F . . . 9.46 inches

Winter

December, 41°F; January, 41°F; February, 41°F . . . 9.05 inches

TOURING INFORMATION. There is no shortage of colorful and useful pamphlets, maps, and brochures on the Virginia Peninsula and the Historic Triangle — Jamestown, Williamsburg, and Yorktown. The state of Virginia alone publishes more than 600 separate pieces of information, many of them dealing with the Peninsula and its attractions. To aid you in your advance planning, the following are addresses and telephone numbers of the agencies and organizations that produce and distribute a wide variety of valuable printed material. When writing or calling for assistance, list your primary interests, so the tourism offices can send you the most appropriate material.

Jamestown

The Jamestown-Yorktown Foundation, Box JF, Williamsburg 23187; 229–1607.

Superintendent, Colonial National Historical Park, Box 210, Yorktown 23690; 898–3400.

Williamsburg

Colonial Williamsburg Foundation, Box C, Williamsburg 23187; 229–1000.

Colonial Williamsburg Reservations: (Accommodations) Reservation Manager, Box B, Williamsburg 23187; (800) 446–8956. (Dining) Reservations, Box B, Williamsburg 23187; 229–2141.

Colonial Williamsburg Tour Group Sales, Box 627, Williamsburg 23187; 229–1000.

Colonial Williamsburg Group Marketing Department, Box C, Williamsburg 23187; 229–1000, Ext. 2435.

Yorktown

The Jamestown-Yorktown Foundation (see Jamestown above).

Superintendent, Colonial National Historical Park (see Jamestown above).

Yorktown Victory Center, Box 1976, Yorktown 23690; 887–1776

Around the Virginia Peninsula

Peninsula Chamber of Commerce, Coliseum Mall A-12, 1800 W. Mercury Blvd., Hampton 23666; 838–4182.

Hampton Information Center, 413 W. Mercury Blvd., Hampton 23666; 727–6108.

Newport News Department of Recreation, Parks, and Public Relations, City Hall, Newport News 23607; 247–8451.

The Williamsburg Area Tourism and Conference Bureau, a division of the Williamsburg Chamber of Commerce, Drawer GB, 901 Richmond Rd., Williamsburg 23187; 253–0192.

Williamsburg Hotel/Motel Association. Call toll-free in Virginia (800) 582–8977, or out-of-state (800) 446–9244.

Busch Gardens, the Old Country, Drawer FC, Williamsburg 23187; 253–3350.

Virginia Division of Tourism, Administration Office, 202 N. Ninth St., Suite 500, Richmond 23219; 786–4484.

Virginia Department of Highways and Transportation, 1221 E. Broad St., Richmond 23227; 786–2702.

Virginia Travel Council, 7619 Brook Rd., Box 15067, Richmond 23227; 266–0444.

HIGHWAY INFORMATION CENTERS. There are Welcome Centers, where the above-mentioned brochures and information may be obtained, just inside the state line on some U.S. highways and on each interstate highway that enters Virginia. They are located as follows: **U.S. 13,** Accomack Co., .8 miles S of VA-MD line; **I–64,** Allegheny Co., 2.6 miles E of VA-WV line; **I–66,** Prince William Co., .3 miles W of Bull Run; **I–77,** Carroll Co., .3 miles N of VA-NC line; **I–77,** Bland Co., .9 miles S of Rte. 606; **I–81,** Frederick Co., 4.2 miles S of VA-WV line; **I–81,** Washington Co., .3 miles N of VA-TN line; **I–85,** Mecklenburg Co., .7 miles N of VA-NC line; **I–95,** Spotsylvania Co., 1.8 miles S of **U.S. 17;** and **I–95,** Greensville Co., .1 mile N of VA-NC line.

TIME ZONE AND AREA CODE. Virginia is in the Eastern Standard Time Zone and goes on and off Daylight Saving Time with the rest of the nation — "springing ahead" in spring, and "falling back" in fall. The Virginia Peninsula has the 804 telephone area code, as does Richmond to the northwest and Norfolk-Virginia Beach to the southeast. Unless otherwise specified, all telephone numbers in this guidebook are in the 804 area.

EMERGENCY TELEPHONE NUMBERS. Although it is our wish and yours that your visit to the Jamestown, Williamsburg, and Yorktown area will be carefree from arrival to departure, the following are useful numbers in and around the Historic Triangle to have on hand in case of emergency.

Jamestown

James City County POLICE	911
James City County AMBULANCE	911
James City County FIRE DEPARTMENT	911

Williamsburg

Williamsburg POLICE	229–1544
Colonial Williamsburg SECURITY	229–1000, Ext. 2600
Williamsburg AMBULANCE	229–1313
Williamsburg FIRE DEPARTMENT	229–1313
Williamsburg Community HOSPITAL	253–6005

Yorktown

York County POLICE	898–0222
York County AMBULANCE	898–0111
York County FIRE DEPARTMENT	898–0111

General

Virginia STATE POLICE	253–4923
Park Rangers	898–3400

 TIPS FOR BRITISH VISITORS. The historic Virginia Peninsula, especially Jamestown, Williamsburg, and Yorktown, is of special interest to many British citizens, for here was the beginning, middle, and end of Britain's New World Adventure, at least insofar as these United States were concerned. British visitors should note the following when planning a trip to the United States.

Passports. You will need a valid passport and U.S. visa (which can only be put in a 10-year passport). The type and validity of U.S. visas vary considerably; detailed information should be obtained from the nearest U.S. embassy or consulate. You can obtain your visa either through your travel agent or directly from the United States Embassy, Visa and Immigration Department, 5 Upper Grosvenor Street, London, W1 (01–499 5521).

Vaccinations. Not required for entry into the United States.

Customs. If you are 21 or over, you can take the following into the United States: 200 cigarettes, or 50 cigars, or three pounds of tobacco (combination of proportionate parts permitted); and one U.S. quart of alcohol. In addition, every visitor, including minors, is allowed duty-free gifts up to a value of $100. No alcohol or cigarettes may be included in this gift exemption, but up to 100 cigars are allowed. Do not take in meat or meat products, seeds, plants, or fruits. Avoid narcotics like the plague.

Insurance. We heartily recommend that you insure yourself to cover health or motoring mishaps with Europe Assistance, 252 High Street, Croydon CROINF (01–680 1234). Their excellent service is all the more valuable when you consider health-care costs in the United States today.

Air Fares. We suggest that you explore budget flight possibilities — APEX and other fares offer considerable savings over the full price. Quite frankly, only business travelers who don't have to watch the price of their tickets fly full price these days — and they often find themselves sitting right beside APEX passengers! You may want to look into available fly-drive programs offered by firms such as Thomas Cook and Trans World Airlines.

HINTS TO THE MOTORIST. The speed limit in Virginia, as elsewhere in the United States, is 55 miles per hour. Note, however, that town and city speed limits are considerably lower, especially in and around historic sites. State law permits a right turn on a red signal, *after a full stop,* unless otherwise directed. Virginia police authorities strictly enforce the state's drunk-driving law. A .01 percent reading of alcohol in the blood constitutes drunkenness. If you're driving a long distance to reach the Virginia Peninsula and belong to AAA or another auto club, they will be glad to provide information about the best routes and to help you plan accommodations during layovers. If you're not an auto club member, a bound volume of maps of the U.S. Highway system, such as those published by Rand McNally, Hammond, and Hagstrom, is a good investment, since gas stations no longer provide free road maps. Maps are also available from the State of Virginia (see above, Touring Information).

DRINKING LAWS. In 1968, the state legislature passed a law permitting by-the-drink liquor service, the most radical change in the state's Alcoholic Beverage Control (ABC) laws since 1934. The law permits "qualified establishments" — meaning bona-fide restaurants, not saloons — to serve mixed alcoholic beverages, subject to local option. Licensed restaurants may serve such drinks until 2 A.M.

TIPS FOR DISABLED TRAVELERS. Virginia, which plays host to hordes of visitors every year, has made significant strides in adapting its attractions to the needs of the disabled. A helpful brochure, "Tips For The Disabled Traveler," is available from Division of Tourism, 202 N. Ninth St., Suite 500, Richmond, VA 23219; (804) 786–2051. *Note:* Many restored Colonial Williamsburg buildings have not been modified for wheelchairs.

SENIOR CITIZEN DISCOUNTS. In some cases, senior citizens may receive special discounts on lodgings. The Days Inn chain offers various discounts to those 55 years and older. Holiday Inns extend a discount to NRTA members (write to National Retired Teachers Association, Membership Division, 215 Long Beach Blvd., Long Beach, CA 90802, if you qualify), and to AARP members (write to American Association of Retired Persons, Membership Division, 215 Long Beach Blvd., Long Beach, CA 90802). The amounts and availability of such discounts change, so it's wise to check in advance with these organizations or the hotel chain. The National Council of Senior Citizens, 925 15th Street N.W., Washington, DC 20005, is always working to develop low-cost travel opportunities for its members, as well.

SUGGESTED READING. For those who like to do a bit of "homework" before visiting a place, a deeper and broader understanding of what Virginia was, is, and has to offer can be obtained from the following books: *Virginia: A Guide to the Old Dominion* (Oxford University Press, NY, 1940) is part of the America Guide Series and is recommended for historical and general background information; *Virginia* by Hans Hannau (Doubleday, Garden City, NY, 1966); *Virginia Beautiful* by Wallace Nutting (EPM Publications, McLean, VA, 1974); and for that very special flavor of dining in Virginia, *Virginia's Historic Restaurants* by Dawn O'Brien (John F. Blair, Publisher, Winston-Salem, NC, 1984). Worth noting for the Colonial Williamsburg segment of your visit to the Historic Triangle is the *Official Guide to Colonial Williamsburg*, which may be ordered in advance for $4.50 from Colonial Williamsburg, 201 Fifth Ave., Box CH, Williamsburg, VA 23187. Order by title and #47076, with a check payable to Colonial Williamsburg. The Foundation, which publishes a number of titles about Colonial Williamsburg, will send you a complete list of publications upon request. Write to Colonial Williamsburg at the above address.

ABOUT OUR MAPS. It goes without saying that the editors and writers of Fodor's Travel Guides strongly advocate the value and frequent use of travel guidebooks to expand and enrich the travel experience. A concise, comprehensive, and *portable* travel guidebook is one of the most valuable items you can pack for a trip — *almost* as essential as your wallet, *more* essential, by far, than your hairdryer or travel iron.

We feel much the same about maps.

Traveling anywhere, we believe, without an accurate, detailed, up-to-date map is like flying with only one wing.

We wouldn't do it — and neither should you.

In preparing this guide to the Historic Triangle — Jamestown, Williamsburg, and Yorktown — our editors and cartographers have devoted considerable research time and editorial effort to providing you, the reader-traveler, with the orientation maps that appear elsewhere in this book. These maps are as comprehensive as space permits — and *that* is our message: the maps throughout this book are for orientation only, nothing more, nothing else. They are meant to "put you in the picture," to give you an overview of where you are, where you're going, and where you may want to go from there.

Our maps, therefore, are meant only to supplement our text as illustrations to complement the Story and the Experience of Jamestown, Williamsburg, and Yorktown.

This brings us to our second advocacy: Travel — *explore!* — with the latest Fodor's guide in one hand and a good large-scale map in the other. With these as your companions, you'll seldom go astray.

A number of excellent maps on Virginia, the Virginia Peninsula, and the Historic Triangle are available free or at a modest cost. Among the best are the following:

Virginia, Seasons of Adventure map. (Free) A detailed road map of Virginia, complete with photos and points of interest, as well as large-scale inserts on Norfolk, Hampton, and Newport News, plus the Jamestown, Williamsburg, and Yorktown area. Available at Virginia Welcome Centers (above); The Bell Tower, 101 N. Ninth St., Richmond, VA, or by writing to Virginia Division of Tourism, Administration Office, 202 N. Ninth St., Suite 500, Richmond, VA 23219.

Map of Williamsburg, James City County, Yorktown, and York County. (Published at $1) Large-scale maps, printed on both sides, of the total Historic Area — Colonial National Historic Park (Jamestown and Yorktown) and Colonial Williamsburg. Contact Williamsburg Area Chamber of Commerce, Drawer HQ, Williamsburg, VA 23187.

Visitor's Companion Map, Colonial Williamsburg. Printed in color, on one side, this detailed map of the Historic Area shows places of interest and bus routes. Available at Colonial Williamsburg Visitor Center and Information Station on Merchants Square.

Touring Maps to Jamestown and Yorktown. Available free in Colonial National Historic Park, the Visitor Centers at Jamestown Festival Park and Yorktown Victory Center, or by contacting the Jamestown-Yorktown Foundation, Box JF, Williamsburg, VA 23187. An *Encampment-Battlefield* map is available free at Yorktown Visitor Center.

 SEASONAL EVENTS. It is difficult to imagine a day when something special hasn't been planned at one or another site in the Historic Triangle; to list them all, a year or more in advance, would require a separate book. Colonial Williamsburg alone publishes three advance calendars covering six months and three months, as well as *This Week in Colonial Williamsburg,* a small informative folder available to visitors. Events range from modest lectures to holiday extravaganzas. The following is a list of annual events by month.

February. Special Williamsburg "package" Colonial Weekends, this month and next, featuring banquet, lectures, and tours. Annual Williamsburg Antiques Forum, including lectures, tours, and social events, early in the month. Washington's Birthday Weekend.

March. Learning Weekend, study of crafts and architectural detail, held in the Historic Area. George Washington's Birthday holiday period celebrated in Williamsburg with a costumed military review. Colonial Weekends, beginning in February, continue through the first weekend in March. Canadian visitors are honored with a parade and special events during Williamsburg's annual Canada Time.

April. Special Historic Garden Week tours in Colonial Williamsburg.

May. Jamestown's Settlement Day Celebration (May 12) features special events and tours. In Williamsburg, the 13 original colonies are honored weekly, mid-May through early July, in a Prelude to Independence celebration.

June. Prelude to Independence Festivities held weekly in Colonial Williamsburg on Market Square green.

July. Colonial Williamsburg celebrates the Fourth of July with fireworks and a stirring parade. A golf tournament, the Anheuser-Busch Classic, is held later in the month. The Prelude to Independence celebration is held early in the month. Hampton holds an Old Hampton Arts and Crafts Festival in mid-June and a three-day Jazz Festival late in the month.

September. Senior Time salutes visitors 55 years and older, with special rates for accommodations, meals, and shopping. Colonial Williamsburg activities include special tours and programs. In late September, Publick Times and Fair Days re-creates a Colonial fair and market, with auctions, military reviews, and craft displays. The Williamsburg Scottish Festival is held the third week of the month at the College of William and Mary.

October. Yorktown Day commemorates the surrender on Oct. 19, 1781, of British forces at Yorktown, with a ceremony and parade. Newport News schedules its annual Fall Festival over two weekends in October.

November. Thanksgiving Weekend in Williamsburg is a family celebration, featuring drama, music, religious events, and special children's tours, plus special holiday dinners at Colonial Williamsburg's taverns and restaurants.

December. The Christmas holiday season (two weeks) opens in Colonial Williamsburg with the Grand Illumination of the Historic Area, and music and entertainment on Duke of Gloucester Street.

 PLACES TO STAY. While there are bargains to be had, and an occasional rip-off, you generally get pretty much what you pay for. This is especially true in a highly competitive touring area like the Historic Triangle, where there is a large selection of accommodations in a wide range of prices. Although prices here tend to be higher than in rural, low-traffic areas, the price structure in and around the Historic Area is fairly uniform and not out of line with major East Coast urban centers.

The key to selecting the *right* place for you to stay is "balance" — that is, balancing your needs, desires, and preferences against your ability or willingness to pay. If you insist on a central location, be prepared to pay extra for the convenience. On the other hand, if location is not important to you, you'll probably enjoy substantial savings. Keep in mind that the major attractions on the Peninsula are not all that far apart, and you'll probably have your own ground transportation anyway.

If you prefer full-service accommodations (restaurants, lounges, room service), again be prepared to pay extra. Here, you should be aware that most hotels and motels are near or adjacent to restaurants, sometimes (along Richmond Road, U.S. 60W, for example) in clusters that are interspersed with a wide variety of eating places, ranging from gourmet establishments to pancake houses.

If an accommodation's ambiance and amenities are important to you, recognize in advance that you'll pay for those, too. But if "a view of the garden" and extra-large and fluffy bath towels rank low on your list of priorities, your travel dollars will almost certainly stretch a bit farther. Whatever your preference, reserve your accommodations well in advance, especially during peak seasons. Weighing what you want against what you'll pay is good travel insurance against future disappointment.

In the first chapter of our Practical Information section, you will find a fairly comprehensive selection of Places to Stay. These selections are arranged alphabetically under separate general location headings in and around the Historic Triangle or elsewhere on the Virginia Peninsula. Each of the listings has one or more of the following general price designations: *Deluxe,* $100 or more; *Expensive,* $75–$100; *Moderate,* $40–$75; and *Inexpensive,* under $40. This *very general* pricing structure is based on double occupancy for one night.

Most major hotels and motels accept major credit cards; others may accept a few or none at all. Many of our listings include those cards that are acceptable at a particular hotel, motel, or chain. These are indicated by the following abbreviations at the end of each selection:

> AE — American Express
> CB — Carte Blanche
> DC — Diners Club
> MC — MasterCard
> V — Visa

If none is listed, the omission may be ours, but it's also possible that the place where you hope to eat or stay has a cash-only policy. Ask *before* you commit yourself.

A few additional words of caution are appropriate here:

• Our selection of listings, while fairly comprehensive, is not complete; new facilities are added each year, while others go out of business or change their names. If you discover an exceptional place that we've overlooked, we would be delighted to hear about it. By the same token, if you disagree with any of our selections, we would appreciate hearing that, too. Our aim throughout is to give you the widest possible choice of locations, facilities, services, and prices — but we are realistic enough to know that it's impossible to please every traveler every time; the best we can do is try.

• Our pricing structure — *Inexpensive* through *Deluxe* — is a general one. Rates may change seasonally or at the discretion of management, and a facility listed in one price category may slip into another while we're on press or before you read or use this guide. Even service may slip, or improve, sometimes in less than a year.

• Although our four general price ranges are based on current lodging trends, plus our years of personal experience, each of us differs as to what we need, what we will pay, and whether we truly believe that where we sleep and change our clothes is really all *that* important. Only you can make those decisions. We can, as we have done, provide broad guidelines, recognizing that a moderate price to one traveler may seem wildly extravagant to another or "a real bargain" to yet a third.

• Each of our hotel-motel-campground listings includes addresses and telephone numbers (often toll-free 800 numbers). Because these numbers are possibly the most valuable part of the total listing, we recommend you make use of them by calling for more details than our abbreviated descriptions can provide. Above all call well in advance to make a firm reservation. The time and money spent before your trip can save you hours — even days — of aggravation later. In fact, it just might *make* your trip!

 TIPPING. Whom to tip, how much, and when, are some of the more confusing aspects of travel. There are no written laws or hard-and-fast rules to govern the practice — merely custom and our own inclination. Unlike much of Europe, where a service charge is added automatically to most restaurant (and some hotel) bills, few restaurants in the United States have adopted this practice. In the rare instance where one has, that fact should be noted on the menu and again on your final bill. When in doubt, *ask;* you may add to the tip, but you are not expected to pay double. Fifteen percent of your total food and beverage bill (excluding any tax) is still universally acceptable throughout the United States, and this, of course, includes the area in and around the Historic Triangle and elsewhere on the Virginia Peninsula. In general, tip as you would at home. Since the virtual disappearance of the half-dollar coin, a dollar bill per suitcase is appropriate for bellhops, or for the doorman who makes an extra effort to hail and help you into a cab. However, if there is a long line of waiting cabs, 25 or 50 cents is sufficient for the simple task of helping you into a taxi. For a local cab ride, 15 to 20 percent of the fare is a reasonably generous tip, and it may even earn you a smile. Many establishments add a fixed room-service charge, usually 10 to 15 percent. It is not out of line to add a bit extra, especially for prompt and courteous service. And finally, there are those unsung and often neglected heroines (and an occasional hero) — the housekeepers and chambermaids who make up your bed, collect your trash, and straighten your room. A tip for a special service performed on request is not inappropriate, and if your stay was especially pleasant, leaving a modest monetary gift when you check out is a nice way to show your appreciation.

 PLACES TO EAT. The Virginia Peninsula is rich in both excellent places to eat (in all price ranges) and in its variety of splendid foods. The traditional cuisine in and around the Historic Triangle is a unique blend of Southern, Colonial, and Chesapeake. There is more truth than hyperbole in the claim that Virginia is a land of plenty, known for its ham, beef, chicken, and seafood. Many time-tested Colonial dishes, such as spoon bread, are still served; filet mignon stuffed with oysters and Brunswick stew are also regional specialties.

Anchored, as it is, with its lower shores on Chesapeake Bay, the Virginia Peninsula is famous for its seafood. It is said, with good reason, that any good Tidewater chef can prepare Chesapeake crab at least 20 different ways, each of them a delight to the palate. Hampton proudly calls itself the "Seafood Capital of Virginia," but this doesn't mean that fine fin-and-claw menus won't be found elsewhere on the Peninsula, nor does it denigrate traditional Southern or Colonial cooking.

Immediately following Places to Stay, in the Practical Information section of this guidebook, is a selection of Places to Eat in and around the Historic Triangle, and nearby on the Peninsula. We don't claim that our lists of selections are all inclusive; instead, we have attempted to provide a broad and well-rounded selection of "safe" places to eat — a varied selection that hopefully will satisfy every taste and pocketbook.

Much said about hotels and motels in the section above also holds true for restaurants, but with one notable difference. While most of us consume three meals a day, we sleep only once. Optimists say this three-to-one ratio improves our chances for choosing well, while pessimists argue it merely increases our chances for choosing badly. Each, *we* think, has it wrong. We feel that dining out — breakfast, lunch, or dinner — is as important a part of the total travel experience as your choice of accommodation, and should seldom be left to chance. It may be unrealistic to expect that each of our three daily meals can or should be a culinary delight, but neither should any of those meals be a disaster. Here, as in choosing the right place to stay, the key to a wise choice is weighing your needs and desires with your ability and willingness to pay. Before you jump to the conclusion that we are placing too much emphasis on money, we hasten to add: We also believe that a well-cooked, well-served order of pancakes and sausage in pleasant surroundings can be every bit as satisfying as a savory cut of beef served in an historic tavern. It all depends on *what* you want, and *when* you want it, whether its a quick-and-easy meal on the go, or a leisurely dining experience.

Our restaurant listings, although abbreviated, include addresses and telephone numbers, as well as the following general price designations: *Deluxe,* $25 or more; *Expensive,* $15–$25; *Moderate,* $7–$15; and *Inexpensive,* under $7. Most of the selections also include one or more credit card designations — AE, CB, DC, MC, or V. But be aware that all establishments reserve the right to change their minds, and a credit card that was acceptable when we compiled our lists may not be acceptable later. When in doubt, ask when you reserve a table or before you sit down to dine.

Restaurants in and around the Historic Triangle are in business primarily to serve the touring public, and there is neither joy nor profit in turning away potential customers. Yet, as anywhere else, this is occasionally necessary, much to the regret of the restaurant's staff and the chagrin of the disappointed customer. Rejection, if it amounts to that, may result from two sources: lack of a reservation or improper attire. Some restaurants accept credit cards, others do not; some restaurants insist on advance bookings, while others won't accept them; and some restaurants are fussy about their customers' dress, while others couldn't care less. Wherever possible, we have tried to give you the guidance you need, but keep in mind that rules sometimes change, and a phone call in advance is a wise move.

THINGS TO SEE AND DO. The last chapter in this guide (located before the Index) gives you a comprehensive listing of attractions in and around the Historic Triangle and elsewhere on the Virginia Peninsula. Although the Triangle is center-stage throughout this Heritage Guide, and the spotlight is focused on America's Colonial period, our listings under Things to See and Do recognize the fact that there are numerous nonhistorical attractions on the Peninsula. The capsule descriptions in this book's concluding chapter are meant to complement Chapters 1 and 2 — The Story and The Experience of Jamestown, Williamsburg, and Yorktown. Wherever possible, these abbreviated listings include hours, admission fees, addresses, and telephone numbers. Following the style set forth in the other Practical Information chapters, our listings are presented alphabetically under the following subheadings:

- Jamestown
- Colonial Williamsburg
- In and Around Williamsburg
- Yorktown
- Hampton
- Newport News

TOURS AND TRANSPORTATION. The following are some organizations that offer tour services for groups or individuals. Call or write for detailed information well in advance of your planned visit to the Historic Triangle or Virginia Peninsula: **Airport Limousine Service,** cars, coaches, and vans, Norfolk International, 857–1231, or on the Peninsula, 877–9477; **Colonial Williamsburg,** Group Sales, Colonial Williamsburg Foundation, Box 627, Williamsburg 23187, (800) 446–8956; **Gallop Tour Service,** tours, guides, and conventions, 220–1615; **Newton Bus Service, Inc.,** Rte. 1, Box 77, Gloucester 23061, tours and charters, 874–2912 or 874–3100; **Robinson Tour and Guide Service,** 8 Foxcroft Rd., Williamsburg 23185, groups or individual touring in the Historic Triangle area, 229–5020; **V.I.P. Celebrity Limousine Corp.,** airport or touring transportation, from vans to Rolls Royces, Fort Magruder Inn and Conference Center, U.S. 60E, Williamsburg 23187, 220–1616 or Norfolk International Airport, 490–1237; **Winn Bus Lines,** Inc., charters and tours, 220–1136.

THE STORY
AND THE
EXPERIENCE

THE STORY

Colonial America Then

by
ELEANOR H. LOUTTIT

"Wot's in it fer me?"

"Och, lad, a Paradise! A veritable Eden where Game and Fish and all manner of Harvest appear as if by Magick! No tax-gatherers, no Sheriffs; only Gold and Good Weather."

Thus were they convinced; those poor farmers, those indifferent apprentices, those younger-son gentlemen, and those sailors who went anywhere a ship took them. The several convicts in the group had not been convinced; they had been shipped. There were 144 men aboard the *Susan Constant,* the *Godspeed,* and the *Discovery* as the outgoing

19

morning tide on December 20, 1606, carried them away from the farewells of their sponsors on the dock.

Captain Christopher Newport, commander of the little fleet, had chosen to sail southwest from England, between the Azores and the Canaries, then due west across the Atlantic, following the route that Columbus had taken more than a hundred years before. Winter passage across the mid-Atlantic is never easy, and this one was not an exception. It took the usual three months, and there were the usual casualties from the usual causes: dysentery, ague, and misadventure. In March they cruised the waters of the West Indies, warm at last, but only able to make surreptitious landfall. This was Spanish enemy territory, and they were to settle themselves well north of it. To the north they turned, and by mid-April they entered the Chesapeake Bay. The three ships, trip-weary and provision-scarce, crawled into the Bay, tiptoeing past the resident Indians as it were. A month later, they sighted a river — a broad, deep fresh river, pouring itself into the bay around a wooded peninsula. Captain Newport ordered the three ships to be moored in six fathoms off the shore.

First things first, they named the river and the peninsula after the king. It was now the "James River" and "James Cittie." Thirty-nine of the original crew died on the five-month passage, but for the remaining 105, fresh water and solid ground were all they needed. The night of May 14, 1607, brought their first peaceful sleep aboard ship and certainly the most rest from labor any of them had had since they agreed to emigrate.

Landfall, at Last

The next morning dawned with the bright freshness of an English May day, and they eagerly rowed the few hundred yards to shore. It certainly looked like Eden — a beach, trees, flowers, grass, birds — a veritable Paradise! Why, even as they pulled their boats onto the sandy shore, they saw a hare dart to the safety of the trees from the edge of the grassy slope behind the beach. They followed the hare slowly, exhilarated by the sweet smell of wild strawberries crushed underfoot as they walked. True, there was a lot of bramble, but bramble usually meant abundant berries and small game. There were trees, by 'r Lady, there were trees! Enough to build a town, enough to warm many a winter, more trees than many of their city-bred fellows had ever dreamed there could be! In fact, one *could* say it was a dense forest.

They had ventured only a little way into the forest before common sense prevailed. Captain Newport and the parson (who *may* have come for the glory of God), remembering that there were other human inhabitants in this land, organized a search for fresh water and a safe place to set up camp. Both were easy tasks — there was only one good, relatively bare area to build on and, as they fanned out along the bank, the water came to them — up around their boots, in fact. Swamp water! Marsh! Had there been mosquitoes in Eden?

Someone mentioned the gold that must be in the hills they thought they could make out in the northwestern distance. When they found that gold, their worries would be over. They could go home.

That night they returned to the boats and, in their excitement, sleep was light for all of them. In the fading twilight, one man thought he had seen an Indian crossing the beach further along the shore. Probably not, but. . . . Then, as darkness gathered at the river's edge, the noises of the night began. Insects hummed, owls screeched, a fox barked, and *other things* proclaimed their presence with weird noises. Eden had had some unknowns, too.

JAMESTOWN

The first task in the following days was to build a place of safety on land. A wooden stockade, rough-hewn and small, went up quickly in a flurry of activity that eased the tensions caused by the night noises and soothed the nagging doubts that they had, indeed, arrived in Paradise. They worked hard — for a little while. They built a few crude houses for shelter and, after debate, bickering, and argument, elected a council. One member was a certain John Smith who had shown on the voyage that he had very definite ideas about how things should work.

A "Cittie" Struggles

Apparently it did not occur to this motley band of transplanted Englishmen that here, 3,500 miles from whatever they had called home, they had to become self-sufficient. By the time the raw, wet cold of the peninsular Virginia winter came down, they had used nearly all the supplies they had brought along. By the new year, they were trading desperately with the Indians and, on occasion, stealing from them. The Indians, who hadn't been altogether fond of their new neighbors anyway, made it difficult for them to even venture into the deeper forests for firewood. That winter the settlers hungered, shivered, sickened, and died. Why they didn't harvest the multitudes of fish in the river is unexplainable. Astonishingly, and apparently through lack of leadership, they passed the spring, summer, and fall of 1608 the same way. The winter of 1608–1609 was dreadful, and by spring, two years after they had arrived, the 38 remaining men were packing to go home when a ship commanded by Lord De La Ware (for whom the state was named) arrived with supplies and more colonists for the Chesapeake area. Saved! — for the moment.

Maybe John Smith had been out-voted; maybe he had been biding his time; maybe he just suddenly woke up, but he finally had had enough. Smith declared himself boss, called himself *Captain* Smith, and took over. His plan was nebulous, but it had a single Biblical base: "He that will not work, neither shall he eat" (or be allowed to stay inside the stockade, or have a house, or be helped by the others, etc.). After a fashion, it worked.

Smith insisted that everyone plant an assigned plot of ground, hunt for and cure meat, fish the river and dry the catch, and, preferring to trade with the Indians himself, stockpile that wonderful native grain, corn.

"Well and good," they grumbled, "but we came here because of the riches to be had. What of making money?" So Smith, who had at least the common sense to know that this was not only *not* Paradise but that nothing would be remotely like England again, agreed to try a commercial venture. They shipped sassafras root, a popular "drug" in England, and soon glutted the market. They tried making pitch and tar from the overwhelming abundance of pine trees but their primary market, ships, were too few. They certainly hadn't found any gold. What could they sell?

The Indian Gift

To the community that was finally taking shape on the marshy riverbank, the Indians had become a fact of life. They were a people with a culture and a continuity of life long before the white men came, and they tried to treat the incursion as just another happening in their world. The ways of the white men were certainly strange, sometimes hurtful, and often funny. The Indian shook his head in wonder, laughed, or punished as he saw fit. The Indians did not consider themselves necessarily hostile or inferior, though the settlers considered them to be both. But the Indians *were* a fact of life.

One John Rolfe found himself attracted to the daughter of a chief named Powhatan. There is no record of their courtship, but Rolfe and Pocohantas were married in 1612, and their marriage signaled a truce between the natives and settlers. As a wedding present, the Rolfes were given some of the best of the summer crop of Indian tobacco. It was harsh, strong, and bitter, but it grew better than almost any other plant on the peninsula. Realizing that its use had gained remarkable popularity since Sir Walter Raleigh had introduced tobacco into England almost 30 years before, Rolfe sent his wedding gift to England on the next ship. Meanwhile, he got hold of some seeds of a sweeter Caribbean tobacco and was ready when the London Company sent orders to start exporting the leaf as a money crop.

It could have been a mistake if King James had not been a canny Scot. For years he had railed against the use of "that 'noxious weed," once going so far as to write a pamphlet denying tobacco's medicinal virtues and holding its pleasures to be unhealthy, if not ungodly. When his council pointed out the profit to be made in the tobacco trade, he moderated his views and dropped his campaign, never one to look a gift horse in the mouth.

The colonists soon began to cultivate carefully, to dry the tobacco as it hung in smokehouses, and to sort and grade each leaf for shipment. A commercial crop had been started, and it saved the floundering settlement. Money came in, and with it new settlers — this time energetic laborers with families and servants. Building outside the stockade began; individual farms were marked out and bought by families who planned to stay. Permanent homes of more solid construction were put up to replace wattle and daub or raw clapboard on planned streets and, finally, a church was built.

Seeds of the Future

In the first 10 years of its existence, the Jamestown settlement had seen little in the way of government. They had been too busy just trying to stay alive. A succession of "governors" had been sent by the London Company as their charter dictated. These men had all the power that John Smith had taken upon himself, and they were able men, but most merely visited and then went home on the next ship to "report." In

1619 one governor came to stay. He was Sir George Yeardly, and he soon realized that there was no government here and that he was not able to do the job alone. Orders came from London for him to select two men from each section of the ever-widening colony and to have them meet to set up some rules. Twenty-two men came to the meeting that lasted six days. They met in the new church, called themselves the House of Burgesses, and planted the seeds of Colonial self-government.

It must be remembered that the first men who left England for Paradise did so for riches, not freedom. The families who came over in the next decade did so for survival and benefit, not for a chance to be self-governing. The House of Burgesses met only to enact a few local measures because it was too big a job for one man now that the colonials were moving all over the peninsula and beyond. They knew that they were to imitate all things English and they didn't mind. They knew they had to answer to London for any fault, and they thought it proper. They knew they were to meet just once a year to ensure that things were still going smoothly and they were content. They were an extension of England — everybody knew that. The small difference, which would become a big difference, was that they were elected by *all* the males over 16, not just by landowners. Nobody seemed to notice the divergence from Mother England; they had gotten used to the idea that anyone who pulled his weight could have his say.

Other events were shaping the destiny of the little settlement. In 1622 the truce with the Indians ended savagely when Powhatan's successor, watching the farms spreading deeper and deeper into his territory, retaliated with a swift and brutal massacre of nearly a third of the colonists. To the Indian, a killing raid was meant to "teach" the white man not to interfere in the red man's world; thus the strike was bloody, but short. A sustained war might have done it, but as it was, the settlers just buried their dead, picked up the debris, rebuilt their farms, and pushed even deeper along the rivers. The Indian would be shoved back into eventual oblivion.

A neat system of encouraging economic growth had developed over the first two decades, and by 1636 it was so well established that the colony had at least one man who would today be called a millionaire. Any man who could pay passage for 250 people was granted a large parcel of land known as a "hundred" or a "plantation." Most of these plantations fronted some kind of water access, were ideal for growing tobacco, and needed only many hands to be self-sufficient and very profitable. It wasn't long before a few of those hands were black. Slave traders working the Europe-to-Africa-to-the-Caribbean route opened a new market in Virginia and added a new stratum to Colonial society.

Nor had England been negligent of her distant children. When King James realized the true economic potential in these "western outposts," he graciously relieved the London Company of its charter and declared Virginia a Crown Colony. As such, it deserved all care and protection as did any part of England, was subject to all its laws and customs as was any part of England, and owed a lot of its profits to the Crown. The ties were long and chancy across the Atlantic, but they were unbroken.

WILLIAMSBURG

It is well to remember that in the 17th century, a span of 100 years produced at least four generations. Descendents of those first men, the poor farmers, the indifferent apprentices, the younger-son gentlemen, the sailors, and the convicts — if, indeed, there *were* any descendents — were by the late 1690s truly Virginian, as were the families whose parents and grandparents had arrived on later voyages. They no longer had gruelling hardship, savage threat, or lawless disorder. They lived in real houses, paid real taxes, and had the amenities of life of an English countryside. The difference was that those in Virginia were warmer than their English counterparts for most of the year.

Men with these advantages generally begin looking outward as if to discover even more of the available advantages. The inhabitants of Jamestown and its environs, on the other hand, began to look inward. And what they saw was a rather shiftless, scraggly little town in a bug-infested malarial swamp. People had been so busy going *through* Jamestown to get to the rich land up and down the peninsula that almost the only permanent thing about it had been the meeting house of the Burgesses and that had burned down three times! When, in 1698, the darn thing burned down again, those who made decisions — the Burgesses, the royal governor, several wealthy planters — decided to move the colony's capital. Their choice seems to have been given rare good thought.

How to Make a City

In the early days of Jamestown, an outpost had been built five miles inland on a relatively high ground as defense against Indian attack. It was called Middle Plantation and was a pleasant place, midway between two rivers and free of swamp. Several families must have found it so, because in 1690 there was a village of several houses, some stores, two mills, a church, and a tavern, that beloved gathering place of Englishmen for years untold. It had served as substitute capital during the various times of stress in Jamestown — pestilence, fire, and, once, rebellion. In 1695, the colony's first educational institution, the College of William and Mary, was started there. It had relatively undeveloped acres available and thus was ready for a planned town to be built. Middle Plantation was renamed Williamsburg (for the current king, William III) and, in 1699, it became the capital of the Virginia Colony.

Francis Nicholson, Royal Governor of the Colony of Virginia by appointment of His Majesty William III, was qualified to plan a town. He had already done one — Annapolis — when he was governor of the Maryland Colony. And quite a successful town it was, too.

Nicholson had few physical restrictions in the plans for his new town. The land was higher than most of the area between the rivers, but it was not hilly. Several small creeks drained it well, but they were not of a size to interfere with his proposed layout. At the west end of his sketch pad he drew in the College, its few buildings in place, attractive, and proclaiming "culture!" The roadway for the small settlement that had been Middle Plantation ran up to the doors of the College on a fine east-west axis, so Nicholson had only to draw a straight line, a scaled mile, to the east side of his sketch pad for his town to begin to take form. As a balance to the College, the east end would be the Capitol, the purpose of all this planning. Exactly midway between the two, Nicholson laid out his commercial necessity, the Market Place. Here the town would govern itself (ergo a courthouse), carry on its commerce (ergo wide green spaces for vendors), and marshall its defenses (ergo the Powder Magazine and the guardhouse). The existing church, the Bruton Parish Church (Church of England), found itself to be west of the Market Place and north of the broad main avenue, Duke of Gloucester Street. A fitting place, outside commerce and nearer culture than politics. But just to make sure everyone remembered who was what, Nicholson went about a quarter of a mile north of the town center and sketched in the Governor's Palace.

Both Duke of Gloucester Street and the Palace Green were wide (almost 100 feet) and spacious avenues with commanding views of everything that needed to be seen. Nicholson ruled in several more streets, parallel to and intersecting Duke of Gloucester Street, and almost all of them arrow straight. The rest of the sketch was mostly lines indicating vacant lots waiting for homes and the stores to come.

Of course, Governor Nicholson's tidy plan did not spring overnight into a little living city. Buildings cost labor and money and rose slowly, especially public buildings. When Nicholson completed his plan in

1700, the few buildings of William and Mary College at the west end and the Bruton Parish Church (built in 1683) were the only structures besides the few homes and shops that made up the town. Work was begun on the Capitol in 1701 but before it was completed in 1705, the General Assembly of Virginia was conducting its business there. (The House of Burgesses and the Governor's councillors, royal appointees for life, had long since merged quietly into a two-house Assembly.) The Powder Magazine, important storehouse for weapons of defense and meeting place for the militia was built in Market Square in 1715. The small buttressed brick church of Bruton Parish was unable to accommodate all its parishioners as the town developed, so in 1712 a new cruciform brick building was begun just a few yards from the old church. It was completed in 1715 without appreciably changing Nicholson's plan.

The Crown Jewel

The English Crown still owned Virginia at the turn of the 18th century so it was to be prominently represented by the Royal Governor's residence. The whole colony was made up of small farm settlements, most not even daring to call themselves towns. Even wealthy planters lived in one-story wooden houses, sometimes with only two or three rooms. Only the "very best" had glass in the windows or interior finishes on the walls. As a rule, only public buildings were built of real brick, and there were precious few public buildings in the entire colony. *Impressive* was to be the watchword for the new palace. And impressive it was to most Virginians, when in 1706 the General Assembly appropriated £3,000 towards its erection. (This, after repeated prodding from the London Palace.) For the next five years, work proceeded in a most leisurely fashion until a new governor, Alexander Spotswood, came to Williamsburg. The man seemed to have limitless interests and the vitality to pursue them. When in 1722, the General Assembly balked at further expenditure, Spotswood quit the project cold, and the Governor's Palace was declared finished. It was a real gem to proclaim a crown's presence in the capital. Meanwhile, something new was taking place. A town had been, from the start, a place for meeting others. As a central market for farmers, as a gathering place for leaders, as a base for religion and its succor, as a place to exchange ideas, a town was a meeting center. Even London, in the 1600s had little more to offer. But life was becoming more stable, populations were growing, and productivity was increasing. People were demanding more in their lives —

more clothes, more implements, and more books. Greater numbers of workers were turning to manufacturing and retailing. Commerce joined the traditional educational, religious, and political facets of the town as the age of the consumer began.

In the beginning there were the people connected with the maintenance of an outpost. They were joined by those who had dealings with the College of William and Mary. The small settlement of Middle Plantation had a few houses and shops, two mills, a church, and a tavern. When it became Williamsburg in 1699, the business of government with all its accoutrements moved in. Support people and the members of the governing bodies, Burgesses, councillors, and the Royal Governor, all moved in. Lawyers, of course, followed. One tavern led to three, and shops proliferated. Artisans came and building tradesmen were in great demand. And there were slaves as well. In the 80 years of its vibrant existence as the capital of Virginia, Williamsburg grew from an outpost to a bustling town of nearly 2,000 people — a complex community of pastoral, suburban, and urban elements where the living was good.

YORKTOWN

Early in the conflict that would be called the American Revolution, John Adams probably best described the political climate of the American colonies when he talked about the one-third of the population who were loyal to England, the one-third who shouted for war, and the one-third who didn't give a damn. Those proportions didn't change very much during the seven years of actual fighting. Even the fire-breathing declaimers, such as Sam Adams and Patrick Henry, realized there was no manufacturing, no coinage, no army, and no unity in the colonies. Thirteen separately governed entities, themselves consisting of a myriad of widely spaced smaller entities, were not prepared to wage a real war against a world power such as England. While it was true that England was governing stupidly and selfishly, she could be counted on to overcome these deficiencies if provoked to fight. King George might be 'round the bend, but his ministers and generals were much closer.

It came as a mild but pleasant shock then, when after losing at Lexington and Concord and again at Bunker Hill, the Colonial "army" captured the city of Montreal. A month later they failed to take Quebec. During the next year the Americans' new general, George Washington, was forced to evacuate New York City, but he crushed the Hessian mercenaries in New Jersey and caused the British major-general, Charles Cornwallis, to withdraw from that colony.

The "Different" War

This war was being fought in a pattern familiar in 18th-century Europe — a battle here, a battle there, months of inactivity, and a few hours of bloody fighting. There was no one decisive foray, but unique circumstances that were to decide the outcome. The red-coated British army had for centuries, like all the armies of Europe, stood in close-order drill and fired their rather inaccurate smooth bore weapons at a massed enemy standing in close-order drill firing back. For generations, the American Colonials had been forced to learn the skill of picking off a running deer or flying bird for food or a skulking Indian for survival. They had to be able to fire accurately from the cover of a single tree or while riding a farm horse at a rough gallop. They had even developed a gun that better controlled a bullet's flight by scoring or "rifling" the barrel.

According to one British commander's report to Commons, "These Americans will not stand and fight." Indeed, they didn't. They answered the call for men to fight in a particular place, fought, and then went home to get on with their regular chores. What was needed was a real army. By the time the new government, the Continental Congress, got around to raising one, it had become apparent that what was needed was more involvement by the Southern states in this bid for independence; and so a Virginian was appointed commander-in-chief. He was a gentleman planter, a former explorer of sorts, who had once been a British soldier. The choice of George Washington of Mount Vernon, Virginia, is one of those circumstances that, in hindsight, is called "fortuitous" or "divinely inspired." It turned out, in any case, to be perfect. He was a man of less-than-awesome talent, multifaceted experience, and overwhelming presence, not the presence of money, fame, or achievement, but the complete self-assurance of his own integrity and sense of duty. He led because he felt it was the right thing to do, and men followed for just that reason. Though he was never able to raise an army of more than 18,000 men at one time, neither did he desert the 3,000 who remained with him after that dreadful winter in Valley Forge. He had his own standard of honor, and he lived up to it.

Old Enmities, New Campaigns

The fighting stance, the weaponry, and the super leader all might have been in vain but for the zeal with which France and England continued to pursue their old enmity. While the fledgling United States had been begging France to enter the conflict since early days, France had been dodging its commitment. When the main British force under General Burgoyne was cut off from a rendezvous with General Howe and from retreat into Canada, Parliament was forced to agree to some concessions to the Americans. France recognized a weak moment in English power and entered the war by recognizing the United States as an independent nation and by sending a large army and a powerful fleet. The British had to go on the defensive in America in response to the opening of the front closer to home. Fighting came to a standstill around the major cities of New York and Philadelphia.

The British general, Henry Clinton, commander-in-chief of England's forces, chose to take his operations to the soft underbelly of the colonies and attacked Savannah, Georgia. The city fell, and Clinton marched north to Charleston, South Carolina. The British forces overwhelmed the defenders commanded by Colonel Benjamin Lincoln and humiliated the 5,400 troops who surrendered. Clinton had handed the Americans their heaviest defeat of the war, and he rubbed it in. He declined to recognize the Americans as armed defenders of a sovereign nation; he allowed them none of the traditional honors of capitulation. Smiling in victory and with new impetus for his command, Clinton sailed north and left Charles Cornwallis in command under orders to take no major risks.

Cornwallis didn't. He easily defeated the Americans at Camden, South Carolina, and though suffering a setback at Cowpens, South Carolina, pursued to avenge it at Guilford County Courthouse, North Carolina. There he held his own but gave up pursuit and withdrew to Wilmington, North Carolina.

It is difficult to understand his next move. Perhaps because he considered Savannah, Charleston, and Wilmington safe from all but those annoying gadfly raids by ragtag patriots like Thomas Sumter and Francis Marion, perhaps because he knew supplies and reinforcements could more easily reach the Chesapeake, but whatever his reasoning, he turned his army north and marched to Virginia. He collected small British units along the way, until he had an army of 7,500 men. He turned to the coast in late June of 1781 and chose the tiny port town of Yorktown as a winter base from which he could maintain sea communication with Clinton in New York.

It was now France's turn.

The French Connection

When France entered the war, her army was commanded by General Jean Rochambeau. He placed himself and his troops under Washington's command but instructed his naval commander, Admiral François de Grasse, to handle the French naval contingent at his own discretion. Washington and Rochambeau debated the best course of combined action for their armies and settled, with reluctance on the part of Rochambeau, on a campaign against the British in New York. As they were preparing for an assault on Clinton, they received word from de Grasse that, on August 13, he was taking 24 ships to the Chesapeake Bay. Washington and Rochambeau hastily changed tactics and high-tailed it to Virginia.

In early August, Cornwallis had begun fortifications just southeast of Yorktown along the grassy banks of the York River. He had stationed a small garrison across the river at Gloucester Point north of town and thus assured himself command of the river. He had, then, a naval base to handle his supply lines and communications with Clinton in New York. He had reasonably comfortable winter quarters for his 8,700 men. He and Clinton would have time to discuss the relative merits of a Virginia campaign and a Maryland-New Jersey campaign during the long months before spring.

He could not have known that a decision made by a French admiral in the West Indies that very same month would ruin it all. De Grasse had opted for Chesapeake Bay (instead of New York) as the place to meet the English navy. He got there first and on August 30 set his ships at blockade position literally behind Cornwallis' back. As the 19 British ships under the command of Thomas Graves appeared a week later, de Grasse, after one sharp encounter, kept them maneuvering for three days. When on September 10, the French squadron from Newport sailed onto the scene, Graves chose discretion and sailed back to New York. Cornwallis was sealed off from any help by sea.

A small contingent of American troops, led by another Frenchman, the Marquis de Lafayette, had meanwhile become aware of de Grasse's position. They moved east from central Virginia and were joined by troops from de Grasse's ships. Everyone waited for Washington and Rochambeau who were marching rapidly southward. De Grasse sent ships up the Chesapeake to bring the bulk of those forces to Williamsburg. On September 28, it was all coordinated, and 9,000 American soldiers with 7,800 French allies moved forward to begin the siege of Yorktown.

Siege

Siege operations are, for the most part, a combination of "hurry up" and "wait." The word "siege" comes from an Old French word meaning "seat" and a Latin verb meaning "to settle." And that's just how it works; one finds himself a seat (usually in a hastily dug, uncomfortably muddy trench) and settles in to wait until the enemy's nerve or ammunition gives out, whichever comes first. It's a matter of excruciatingly hurried hard work to dig a trench under the cover of night and then sense-dulling boredom to sit and wait for one of the enemy to be rash enough to show himself. If the trenches can be augmented by artillery pieces, gunners can monotonously pound the places where the enemy is thought to be. This was the situation at Yorktown for the first eight days of the siege.

Cornwallis had pulled his forces into a tight quadrangle around the town, abandoning his outer defenses, on September 30. He had trenches with artillery as a defense perimeter with a series of big guns to protect his seaward rear. He had placed and manned several redoubts (small enclosed defense works or protective barriers) outside his perimeter to the east and south while a squad of fusiliers (sharpshooters with flintlock muskets) protected his western approach. The French and Americans kept up artillery and small arms fire while they moved their armies in closer. On October 6, Washington was ready to squeeze the British by attack. Under the cover of night, the Allies completed a trench from the French battery to the York River, and the next day Washington brought up his field guns to the trench line. They hammered the British defenses, but the battle was give and take, back and forth, until one severe blow caused obvious damage to the British lines. Washington claimed advantage of this opportunity and moved forward to dig a second trench face-to-face, so to speak, with the English defenses. The completion of the second trench was delayed by the fact that British redoubts numbered nine, and 10 were in its direct path. They had to go! On October 14, Washington, with scrupulous fair-mindedness, ordered 400 French troops to attack Redoubt 9 while 400 American troops attacked Redoubt 10. The attack was made during the night and the fighting was hand-to-hand carnage but both hills were taken before dawn. The offensive trench could be completed, and the big guns trundled up to Cornwallis' door.

General Charles Cornwallis was no fool. He made one attempt on October 16 to retake the redoubts. When it failed, he made plans to evacuate his troops across the York River to the Gloucester Point defenses with, he hoped, the protection of the few British ships that lay bottled up in the river. When an Indian summer Chesapeake storm blew up that very afternoon, he sued for peace. On the morning of October 17, 1781, Cornwallis sent his proposal for a truce to the allied commanders.

The tone was set for what would follow when Cornwallis asked for a 24-hour cessation of hostilities and the appointment of a negotiating team. Washington agreed to the truce but gave the English only two hours to decide under what terms they would surrender. It must be pointed out here that the honors of war were serious business once upon a time and that leaders prided themselves on being officers *and* gentlemen. Washington was saying to Cornwallis that he and his men would be treated respectfully but that there would be no fooling around. Accordingly, it was arranged for the negotiators to meet the next afternoon, October 18, at "Mr. Moore's house."

"Terms, Gentlemen . . . "

A little more than a mile down the road from the main battle point, southeast of town and in the middle of a small plantation, was "Mr. Moore's house." The plantation had been worked almost from the beginning of English settlement, but the house hadn't been constructed until the early 1700s. Its owner, Augustine Moore, was a successful merchant who had married Lucy Smith, heiress to the plantation. They and their children lived a quiet life beside the river in the pleasantest of surroundings. It was, then, a rather disagreeable duty to have to concede to the request that they give up their parlor to the four men who were to hammer out surrender terms and to contend with cigar smoke, perhaps, certainly a few glasses of port or sherry, contentious (maybe even blasphemous) language by raised voices, and, probably, muddy booted aides running in and out. "Yes, yes, gentlemen. By all means, be our guests and welcome!"

Shortly after noon, October 18, 1781, four men sat down at a small table near the catercorner fireplace in the Moore's parlor. Colonel Thomas Dundas and Major Alexander Ross were the British team; Colonel John Laurens, the American, with Viscount de Noailles of France, made up the allied team. These four men were commissioned to reach agreement on the formal terms for the surrender of nearly 8,000 English and mercenary Hessian troops to the besieging French-American armies. Theirs was not a pleasant task; sharp exchanges were frequent. Heated arguments, couched in the formalities of protocol and rank, continued until late into the night. The article of surrender that rankled most was Article III, in which the British and their German hired troops were required to shoulder their arms (i.e., appear as a competent army, not as a broken horde), to wrap or encase their company flags (i.e., lose their individual military identity), and to march away to the cadence of their own battle music (be disallowed even to pay respect to the victors). This seemed a bit much to the British team, and they protested such blatant negation of the code of honor for war. These terms were exactly what Colonel Lincoln and his men had been given at Charleston by Clinton on the grounds that the defenders were not an army of a sovereign state but rather were rebels to the British crown. By imposing the same terms at Yorktown, Colonel Laurens was not being petty; he was making the British admit that they were surrendering to a *nation*. Article III was termed "harsh" by both sides, but it stood.

Just before midnight, the truce was extended until 9 A.M. the following day, and the commissioners' report was taken to Washington, who was then camped in Redoubt 10. He made some minor changes and sent the papers to Cornwallis at Yorktown. He and his senior naval officer signed the surrender and sent it back to Washington, who noted the date and place, then signed it. Rochambeau and an aide to de Grasse also signed. It was all over but for the final dramatic scene.

The Last March

'

Between the American encampment and the town lay almost two miles of grassy Virginia fields, shaded oak and maple groves turning to autumn glory, and a dusty road leading south to Hampton. It was on such a green tree-ringed meadow, between two forks of the road, that the final scene would be played.

By the time the first of Cornwallis' soldiers left the town to march in parade columns down the road to surrender, the American troops had been positioned along the route on one side of the road and the French troops along the other. It was between these ranked victors that the proud British regulars, in their red coats with clay-piped straps, and their Hessian comrades would step smartly to a familiar drum beat, "arms shouldered and flags cased." Audible taunts from the sidelines were quickly quelled by quiet orders from the stiffly posed American and French officers. Grins and smirks were not so easily reproved. Many of the somber faces of the marching men were streaked with tears. It was a long walk and at the end lay abasement. As each platoon reached the rectangle, ringed by artillery pieces and cavalry units, the orders came to unshoulder their arms, take one step forward, and, quite literally, *lay down their arms.*

Pile after pile of muskets grew in long rows until the field took on the appearance of one harvested by devastation. Quiet flowed over the ranks as the marching feet came to a standstill and General Charles O'Hara rode forward. He was second-in-command to Cornwallis and had been chosen to perform the actual act of surrender in Cornwallis' place. (There is no record of Cornwallis' whereabouts that afternoon.) Nor did Washington or Rochambeau personally accept the surrender; instead, Major General Benjamin Lincoln, hero of Charleston, victim of British humiliation, and symbol of a turned tide, received the sword from O'Hara.

Wild cheering broke forth from the Americans and the French as the English and Germans were called to rank and began to march from the field. His Majesty's pipers accompanied them away to the old British marching tune "The World Turned Upside Down."

Indeed, it had.

Epilogue

The war had not ended, in fact, but fully a third of the British forces in the Colonies had been lost, and what battles remained were not much more than skirmishes between the patriots and the redcoats. King George's cabinet resigned, and the new one opened peace negotiations that were to take nearly two more years before becoming final.

Amy Harold

THE EXPERIENCE

Colonial America Now

Time travel *is* feasible . . . and in your own automobile, at that. Routes I–64, U.S. 60, and U.S. 17 are the modern, well-kept, and easy-access highways that lead to the middle of the Virginia Peninsula, where it is possible to travel back in time. The road to the past is called the Colonial Parkway. It is a 23-mile scenic drive, inhabited only by other time travelers.

The foremost impression is serenity. The road unwinds gently between stands of tall pines and spreading hardwoods. Intersections are over or under, as a rule, and are outlined with the neat red brick we immediately identify as "Colonial." The road disappears under the three blocks of "town," in no way interfering with the ambience of Williamsburg.

But don't miss the stopping places. View the surroundings from the many overlooks and study the interpretive markers along the route; it will enrich your tour.

There are no service stations along the parkway and no fees are charged, except for those few commercial vehicles allowed on it. It is ranger-patrolled along its entire length, and the speed limit is 45 m.p.h. (72 k.m.h.). There are picnic areas at Great Neck, south of Williamsburg toward Jamestown, and Ringfield, midway between Williamsburg and Yorktown. Camping is not permitted along the parkway but is available in Williamsburg and near Jamestown on Rte. 31.

There are standard highways (VA 31, VA 199, etc.) to drive between the three points of the Historic Triangle but, if you take them, you'll miss a nice ride into the past.

JAMESTOWN

The Jamestown-Yorktown Foundation, an agency of the Commonwealth of Virginia, along with the National Park Service of the Department of the Interior are the administrators for both these sites in the Historic Triangle. The two groups have done commendable work in preserving, restoring, and bringing to life the first permanent English settlement in the New World. There are two distinct areas on the Jamestown site, and they should be visited with distinct goals in mind. The Jamestown Festival Park (a misleading name, perhaps) is a serious exhibit that will set the stage and backlight the action for the experience of the original site. So we begin at the Festival Park.

Just past the Entrance Station is the Visitor Center. Here park interpreters will present a short history of Jamestown and will explain what you are about to see. Even if you have just finished rereading our Story section, please give them your attention. They will prepare you for the "feeling" of the 17th century you are entering.

The park is set up to be a walk through these early times but there is one divergence — the New World Pavilion concentrates (understandably) on Virginia from settlement to statehood. It might be better to save it until last.

Newcomers and Natives

The Old World Pavilion, the first building on the left past the service area, depicts the European background of the settlers, highlighted by

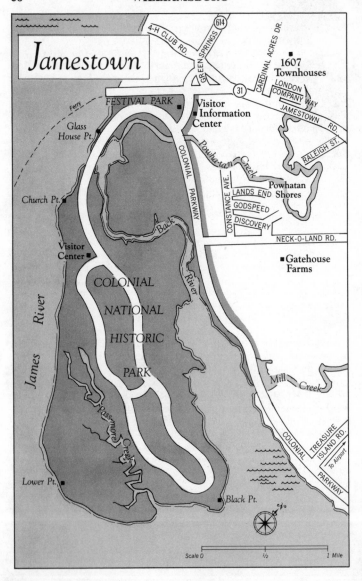

Jamestown

wax figures of three generations of Tudor monarchs who developed the naval power that guaranteed Britain command of the seas, a necessity for successful colonization efforts. There are dioramas, exhibits, and artifacts to pore over. We are here reminded of the great seafarers who ventured out back to find what was literally a new world.

It was not an empty land these early Europeans came to. There were people, nearly 9,000 of them, living harmoniously with the temperate environment in a Stone Age culture. The Tidewater Virginia Indian Village replica (take a right at the first diverging path) offers reproductions of their dwellings and reenactments of their daily lives. The setting is as authentic as possible, though we suspect it is a tad cleaner than those the settlers encountered.

Our path continues to the shore, and there are the *Susan Constant,* the *Godspeed,* and the *Discovery* moored to a pier in a tiny cove. These are not models; they are *exact* reproductions of the ships that sailed from England to Virginia. They are seaworthy, but they are so *small!* Close your eyes as you lean back against a bulkhead and *try* to imagine five months in passage, 144 men, cold and wet days and nights, moldy food, brackish water, and sickness and death.

Shelter and Sustenance

Back on land once more, the path now leads to James Fort, a full acre triangle of land within stockade walls. The fort contains 18 wattle-and-daub buildings: the "buildings of publick necessity" — the church, the storehouse, and the guardhouse — and 15 homes. Wattle-and-daub is a combination of timber framing, woven twigs and branches (wattle) plastered with a mixture of mud and cattle hair (daub). The buildings are thatched; marvelous protection from the elements and marvelous playgrounds for vermin. When you encounter the costumed staff at work in the fort, it is well to remember that they are portraying the life of the settlers *after* the "starveing" time, *after* the arrival of women, and *after* John Smith got going. Just outside the fort, along the return path, is the craft exhibit area. Stop a minute and watch the farmers in their 17th-century garden. The weavers, the spinners, the armorers, the basket-makers — each is really working at the task, and each is a craftsman. Any of the "inhabitants" will be glad to answer your questions or to explain his role. The livestock encountered are domesticated animals, not pets, so be careful about approaching them.

Come slowly back to the present with a visit to the New World Pavilion, then stop at the Mermaid Tavern for refreshment and the

1607, Inc. Gift Shop for a memento of your visit. You're ready now
to visit the Colonial National Historical Site.

"James Cittie"

Jamestown National Historical Site is an island, but barely. Since
1607 it has gradually lost its precarious northern attachment to the
main peninsula. The Colonial Parkway bridges the gap where the
Powhatan Creek and the Back and James rivers meet, so the visitor is
hardly aware that he is crossing onto an island. Much of the island's
shoreline has eroded, leaving the higher middle ground upon which the
settlement grew. The island is green with trees and grass, and the river
is wide and calm. You are on the western shore as you approach the
Visitor Center.

Again, the center is just past the Entrance Station and the car park.
It is a good recap of the things you learned at the Festival Park as well
as a starting point for a tour of the settlement. Park rangers conduct
tours of the site from there if you care for an instructor, but feel free
to walk on your own, if you like. The sights are all well explained by
discreet markers. Visitors can take in the place that has been fixed *by
tradition* as the point on the James that was the site of the first landing
and the first fort. In "New Towne," the area where Jamestown expanded about 1620 (after tobacco money began in earnest), walk along
"Back Street" and other original pathways. Archaeological digs since
1934 have produced streets, monuments, ditches, hedge rows, and
fences as well as house foundations of the 17th-century town that have
been outlined in whitewashed brick. While wattle-and-daub came first
in the fort area, New Towne was of a more permanent clapboard and
brick. In this area are the homesites of Richard Kemp (builder of one
of the first brick houses in America), Henry Hartwell (a founder of
William and Mary College), Dr. John Pott, and William Pierce (who
led the "thrusting out" of Governor John Harvey in 1635), as well as
the sites of Country House and Governor's House.

Remnants and Reminders

The only standing ruin of the 17th-century town is the Old Church
Tower. It is believed to be part of the first *brick* church on the continent

(1636). Today Memorial Church adjoins the Tower. This church was built in 1907 by the Colonial Dames of America over the foundations of the original. Within are foundations said to be those of the earlier church. The foundations of a brick building have also been discovered near the river. These are believed to have been those of the First Statehouse.

There is the Tercentenary Monument near the Visitor Center, built in 1907 to commemorate the 300th anniversary of the colony's founding. Other monuments include the Captain John Smith statue, the Pocahantas Monument, and the House of Burgesses Monument.

Civil War buffs will enjoy inspecting several Civil War fortifications on the island, especially the Confederate Fort, built in 1861, near the Old Church Tower. There also are a few ancient grave markers that are quite difficult to decipher and, thus, quite fascinating to graveyard enthusiasts.

A short walk from the church are the Glasshouse, where costumed craftsmen demonstrate the art of glassblowing, and Dale House, where other craftsmen re-create the style of pottery used in 17th-century Jamestown. You may purchase original pieces here.

WILLIAMSBURG

Williamsburg is normally the star attraction of the Virginia Peninsula. In this guide, dedicated to the Historical Triangle of Jamestown, Williamsburg, and Yorktown, it will be treated as what it originally was — the interim locale between settlement and revolution, four generations in the chrysalis stage; comfortable, unhurried, peaceful living between rugged hardship and the bloody birth of a new country.

That this "in-between" place should be located just about halfway between Jamestown and Yorktown makes keeping to an orderly tour quite easy. After a few hours of absorbing and understanding life in a 17th-century colony, we make a smooth transition to the 18th century at Colonial Williamsburg. One word of caution: The discreet road signs guiding the visitor to the Restoration are somewhat confusing. Though they seem to point every which way, most of them will get you to the Visitor Center, which is the logical starting place. They will *not*, we found, get you to Williamsburg Lodge or Williamsburg Inn if you want

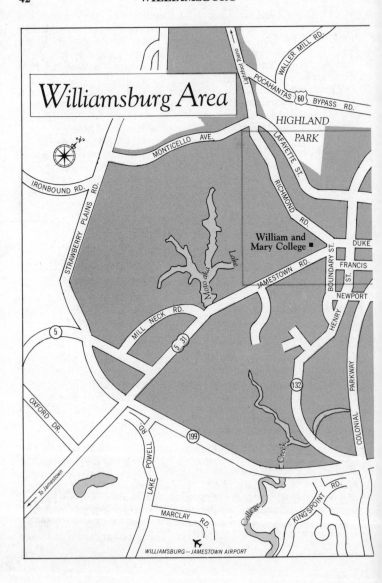

Williamsburg Area

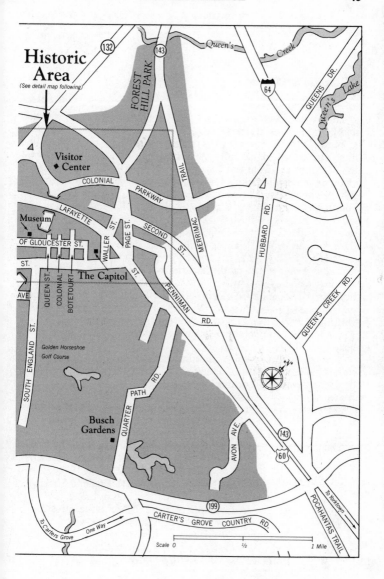

to check in before starting your exploration. The signs that do are practically nonexistent. Follow our map or ask!

The Visitor Center

The Visitor Center is a large complex which includes information and literature kiosks, ticket sales, a reservation service, bookstore, bus stop, car park, rest rooms, and a continuous showing of an orientation film. You are urged, nay, all but directed, to go there first if you want to make the most from your Williamsburg experience. When you purchase an admission ticket, you will be given a choice of a Basic Pass or a Patriot's Pass; the cost difference is about 33 percent. Each allows you free access to the bus service and all the walking around you care to do. With the Basic Pass, however, you will have to pay extra for such exhibits as the Governor's Palace, Bassett Hall, Carter's Grove Plantation, and the DeWitt Wallace Gallery. The Patriot's Pass is good for a whole year, allows you to see everything without additional charge, and adds a mental pat on the back for being a "patriot." The tickets are the single largest source of revenue for the upkeep of the Restoration, the rest coming from charitable gifts, rentals, accommodations, craft sales, and an endowment. (When we were confronted not long ago with the small sign in London's Westminster Abbey that said it costs £2 a minute to maintain the Abbey, the admission price to any genuine historical adventure became modest.)

You cannot drive your car through the Historic Area; therefore, you should take the bus to a starting place such as Stop #1, the Palace, or choose to walk from the Visitor Center. With your pass you can board the bus or disembark at any stop in the Historic Area. The Restoration is about one mile (1.6 km) long and one-half mile (.8 km) wide, with literally hundreds of buildings, homes, and shops to see. Be warned that there is a *lot* of walking to do.

The bus makes 10 stops and runs every few minutes from the Visitor Center and back again (see Bus Stop map). The stops in order are:

#1.   Near the Palace Grounds on North England Street
#2.   Corner of Queen Street and Nicholson Street
#3.   Corner of Boutetourt Street and Nicholson Street
#4.   Waller Street across from Campbell's Tavern
#5.   Entrance to Williamsburg Inn
#6.   Abby Aldrich Rockefeller Folk Art Center
#7.   Entrance to Williamsburg Lodge

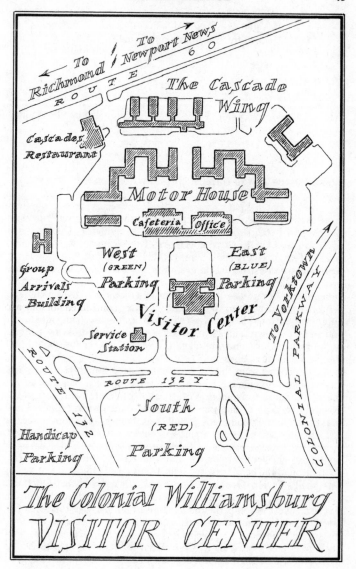

The Colonial Williamsburg
VISITOR CENTER

#7A.   (We can't explain the A) Henry Street near the Public
       Hospital
#8.   Henry Street at Merchants Square
#9.   North England Street at Public Footpath to Visitor
       Center

Assuming your interest in the complete picture of 18th-century life
in the interval between settlement and independence, we outline a tour
that can include everything it is possible to see or that can be as short
as a walk down one street.

The Palace to the Capitol

At the end of the Public Footpath from the Visitor Center or near
Bus Stop #1 stands the Governor's Palace, residence of seven royal
governors and the first two governors of the Commonwealth of Virginia — Patrick Henry and Thomas Jefferson. The Palace, a completely
refurbished reconstruction on the original foundations, is surrounded
by formal gardens, outbuildings, a graveyard, a canal, and a host of
indications that this was, indeed, an impressive place to live. Watch the
Wheelwright at work in the Carriage House; keep an eye and an ear
out for the current "inhabitants" who will be only too glad to chat with
you about the town. Tip: Their speech as well as their dress may belong
to the 18th century, and you may find yourself conversing about "Mr.
Franklin's latest experiment."

As you come out of the Palace grounds, take the street to your left
(east) to North England Street. You'll see Robertson's Windmill across
the street. South to Nicholson Street and then east, you will pass the
Peyton-Randolph House, the Musical Instrument Maker, the Cabinet
Maker, and the Public Gaol.

The latter served the town as a confinement center for common
criminals, a debtor's prison, a detention cell for runaway slaves, a
madhouse, and a military prison. You will pass the jail to Waller Street,
south around the bend, past the Benjamin Powell House to Christiana
Campbell's Tavern; George Washington really did eat here — 10 times
in two months, according to his own diary! Across the street from the
Tavern, take the footpath that leads west to the Capitol. A rather
odd-looking building, the H-shaped Capitol was admirably designed
for a specific purpose. Virginia's General Assembly, bicameral from its
beginning, met here, and the Council sat in chambers on the second
floor west while the House of Burgesses met in a room on the first floor

east. The large conference hall above the arched and open gallery was neutral ground when a deadlock occurred.

Both Sides of the Street

Come out on the west side of the Capitol grounds and step onto Williamsburg's main thoroughfare, Duke of Gloucester Street. Because we find it somewhat frustrating to keep crossing and re-crossing the street, our tour will go one way on the north side and return on the south side. Each building along the street is of some interest and has a name displayed on a discreet plaque. Those which may be visited are the Pasteur and Galt Apothecary Shop, the Raleigh Tavern and Bake shop, the Silversmith, the Milliner, the Grocers Shop, the Printer-Bookbinder and Post Office, Prentis Store, Chowning's Tavern, the Courthouse, the Geddy House and Shop, the Geddy Foundry, and the Bruton Parish Church.

We are now mid-tour at the two-block square modern shopping area, where it is certain you can get lunch. Understandably, the Historic Area cannot and does not cater to casual refreshment. If you wish to dine at one of the taverns, however, it is really imperative that you have a reservation. Don't plan to merely stop in for lunch, dinner, or even a cup of coffee anywhere within the restored area. (Remember, 18th-century innkeepers were rarely confronted by more than half a dozen guests at a time, and *they* put a strain on the facilities. Be pleased that the Foundation strives for authenticity and doesn't sell hot dogs and hamburgers within the Historic Area.)

The tour resumes going east on Duke of Gloucester Street on the south side. Again, many buildings line the street. Those you may wish to visit are the Cooper, Greenhow Store, the Bootmaker, the Powder Magazine, and the Guardhouse where there is often an oxcart making its way across the field from the back street, the Music Teacher's Rooms, the Anderson Blacksmith Shop, the Archaeological Exhibit, Tarpley's Store, Wetherburn's Tavern, the Wigmaker, and the King's Arms Tavern.

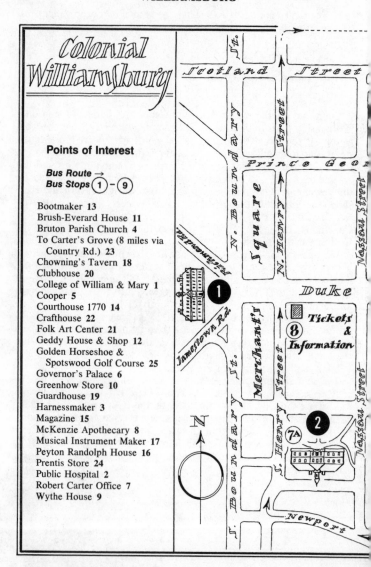

Colonial Williamsburg

Points of Interest

Bus Route →
Bus Stops ①–⑨

Bootmaker 13
Brush-Everard House 11
Bruton Parish Church 4
To Carter's Grove (8 miles via
  Country Rd.) 23
Chowning's Tavern 18
Clubhouse 20
College of William & Mary 1
Cooper 5
Courthouse 1770 14
Crafthouse 22
Folk Art Center 21
Geddy House & Shop 12
Golden Horseshoe &
  Spotswood Golf Course 25
Governor's Palace 6
Greenhow Store 10
Guardhouse 19
Harnessmaker 3
Magazine 15
McKenzie Apothecary 8
Musical Instrument Maker 17
Peyton Randolph House 16
Prentis Store 24
Public Hospital 2
Robert Carter Office 7
Wythe House 9

continued on next page

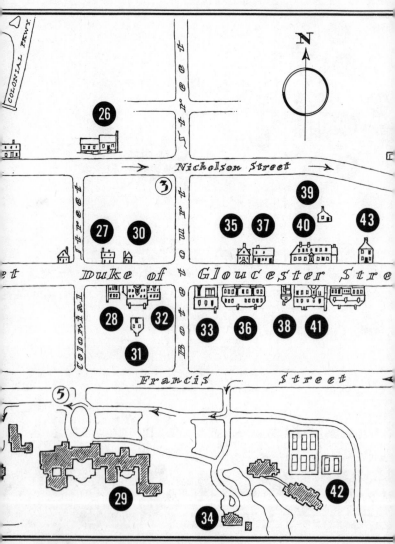

continued from previous page

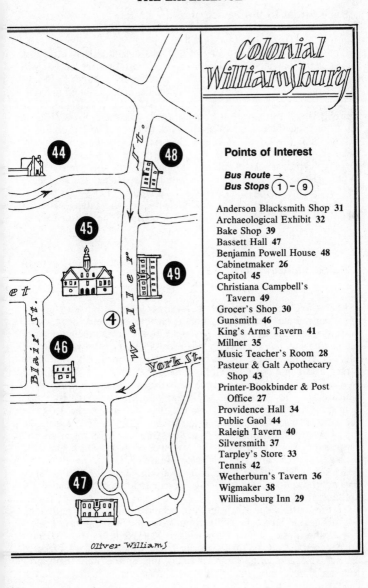

Colonial Williamsburg

Points of Interest

Bus Route →
Bus Stops ① - ⑨

Anderson Blacksmith Shop **31**
Archaeological Exhibit **32**
Bake Shop **39**
Bassett Hall **47**
Benjamin Powell House **48**
Cabinetmaker **26**
Capitol **45**
Christiana Campbell's
  Tavern **49**
Grocer's Shop **30**
Gunsmith **46**
King's Arms Tavern **41**
Millner **35**
Music Teacher's Room **28**
Pasteur & Galt Apothecary
  Shop **43**
Printer-Bookbinder & Post
  Office **27**
Providence Hall **34**
Public Gaol **44**
Raleigh Tavern **40**
Silversmith **37**
Tarpley's Store **33**
Tennis **42**
Wetherburn's Tavern **36**
Wigmaker **38**
Williamsburg Inn **29**

Oliver Williams

Back Street to the Palace

Turn the corner at the east end of Duke of Gloucester Street and continue to Francis Street. Here, if you turn east, on your left you will find the Gunsmith and on your right, the driveway entrance to Bassett Hall, home of Mr. and Mrs. J.D. Rockefeller, Jr., exhibited much as it was when the Rockefellers were in residence. (Special ticket required.) If you turn west on Francis Street, you will enjoy a pleasant stroll past four blocks of restored homes to the Public Hospital and, behind that, the DeWitt Wallace Decorative Arts Gallery. (Special ticket required.) Proceed north on Henry Street or Nassau Street to Duke of Gloucester Street and east to Palace Green. There you can visit Wythe House, the McKenzie Apothecary, the Robert Carter Office, and, across the Green, the Brush-Everard House. Then you're back at the Palace and the path to the Visitor Center or a short step away from Bus Stop #9, the final stop on the return trip to the Visitor Center.

Adjoining Attractions

Everything we've seen so far, with the exception of Bassett Hall and Merchants Square, has been part of the Historic Area of Williamsburg. Just outside the bounds of the restored Colonial town are a number of interesting but not necessarily historical spots. On the west side of Merchants Square (Jamestown Road, Richmond Road, Boundary Street, and Duke of Gloucester Street) is the College of William and Mary. Founded in 1693, it is the second oldest institution of higher education in the United States (Harvard, 1636). The Wren Building, named for Christopher Wren, who may have influenced the design, is the central structure of the College. It was begun in 1695 and is the oldest academic building still in use in America. Flanking it are the President's House (1732–33), the residence of every president of the College save one, and the Brafferton House (1723), originally a residence for Indian students and today housing offices. The three buildings are the epitome of what we have come to know as "Williamsburg architecture."

To the south of the Historic Area, behind Francis Street and along South England Street, lie Williamsburg Inn and Williamsburg Lodge. The Craft House and the Abby Aldrich Rockefeller Folk Art Center are between the inn and the lodge. The lodge, which is also a conference center, is not altogether impressive. The inn, on the other hand, projects an almost immediate "old movie" déjà vu feeling, where even lunch is positively elegant! The Abby Aldrich Rockefeller Folk Art Center (special ticket required) houses a collection of more than 2,000 objects of art created by untutored artisans and offers a changing exhibit along with major loan shows. The Craft House is worth a visit, if for no other reason than to "ooh" and "aah." (Have you ever even imagined a $22,000 breakfront?)

Carter's Grove

Having walked the Historic Area tour, you might have chosen to drive to these above-mentioned sites; it's perfectly possible, and there are car parks at each. You will have to drive or cycle to this next feature, Carter's Grove Plantation. (Special ticket required.) It is located six miles southeast of Williamsburg on the Country Road, the one-way scenic entrance from Williamsburg. The Country Road starts on South England Street and winds through woods and fields, across marshes, and over creeks just as 18th-century roads did. (Return to Williamsburg is via U.S. 60 — it's all well marked.) Carter's Grove Plantation was purchased early in the 18th century by Robert "King" Carter, founder of the rich and influential Carter family, for his daughter, Elizabeth. Her son, Carter Burwell, built the magnificent Georgian mansion dominating the 600 acres that remain of the original plantation. Visitors today can enjoy the house, gardens, orchard, and fine overlook. Don't expect even a glimpse of the Tara image; Carter's Grove is a plantation in the same sense as Monticello.

The land that "King" Carter bought was previously part of a larger tract called Martin's (Merchant's) Hundred. In 1620, a group of English investors built a small town on the riverside, Wolstonholme Towne, and in 1622 a group of peninsular Indians effectively wiped it out. The archaeological remains can be seen today a few hundred yards from Carter's Grove house.

YORKTOWN

At the eastern end of the Colonial Parkway lies the third treasure of American heritage on this 15-mile wide strip of land known as the Virginia Peninsula, the site of the siege of Yorktown. Here, on a tiny battlefield, combined American and French armies forced the surrender of nearly one-third of England's Colonial troops. It was the decisive battle in our war for independence; it marked the end of our beginnings.

Yorktown Victory Center

Here, as at Jamestown, the Jamestown-Yorktown Foundation has built a marvelous complex for your introduction to the historical park. Stop at the Yorktown Victory Center *before* you tour the park for the most rewarding visit possible. As you near the town of Yorktown, watch for area road signs displaying a red, white, and blue square of American, French, and British flags. The Center is west of town and *not* on the Parkway. An overview of the Revolution, done with special opticals, multimedia exhibits, and film, lifts you from the gentle and somewhat genteel aura of Williamsburg to the fever pitch of patriotism that compelled men to offer "their Lives, their Fortunes, and their sacred Honour" to the cause of liberty. There is a growing gallery of artifacts in the Center, and you can watch new ones being dug up, as it were, just three blocks from the Center. Here the Virginia Center for Archaeology is engaged in excavating one of Cornwallis' ships, which was sunk during the battle. A special visitors' pier will enable you to walk out to where the divers are at work.

Yorktown Visitor Center

Prepared for what you are about to see, leave the Victory Center and return to the Parkway. Follow it to its eastern end, the National Park Visitor Center. A relatively quiet center in serene surroundings, this is the place to pick up your battlefield map and explanatory brochure. Generals need maps to fight battles; you need a map to understand where and how they fought. Browse the Center before you go out onto the drive, but save the terrace viewing until you have done the first half of the tour; it will help you to enjoy the second half. The end of this tour is a highly emotional experience, and you may not want to "come back down" too quickly.

The tour of the two-week engagement at Yorktown is easy to follow but, unless you're into *long* hikes, it must be done by car or cycle. The Encampment tour is nine miles long, and the Battlefield tour is seven miles long. There are ample stopping places at each site marker where

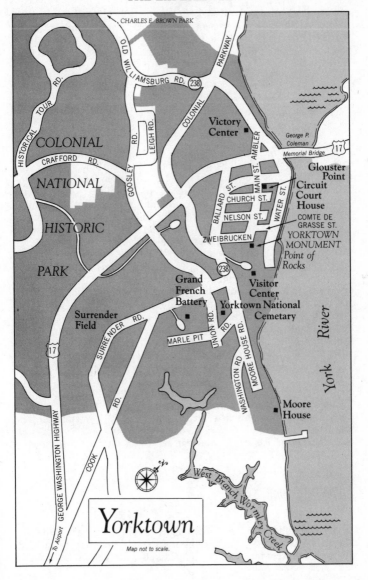

Yorktown

Map not to scale.

you can leave your car and soak up the atmosphere. Even if you don't soak at length, the Encampment tour takes at least 30 minutes and the Battlefield tour at least 45 minutes. It's a good idea to allow yourself half a day or more to see Yorktown, because it was a neatly executed battle with a smash finale!

The Encampment Tour

We strongly recommend that you take the Encampment tour first (see Tour Map). Cornwallis was established at Yorktown in late August when de Grasse blocked his sea access. Washington and Rochambeau did not coordinate all their forces and supply centers until late September. The actual siege forces didn't appear before Cornwallis' lines until the first days of October. The Encampment tour takes you "behind the scenes" to see what the Allies had to set up before they confronted their enemies. The nine-mile drive begins at the Visitor Center parking lot and is marked by YELLOW arrow signs. It runs past open fields, through shady woods, and across a small stream. Along the trail are signs marking sites and explaining their functions: an American and a French artillery park where ammunition was made and baskets for building ramparts and carrying trench soil were fashioned; Washington's headquarters; the French encampment loop (it doesn't require much imagination to "see" soldiers around their camp fires here); a later sad but necessary addition, the French cemetery; and a British redoubt, untouched except by 200 years of nature. The area, unlike a battleground, does not seem alien to our experiences and so, perhaps, helps us get the feel of the battlefield to come. The Encampment tour ends back at the Visitor Center. Take the time to go to the Center's terrace overlook and orient yourself with the arrangement of the battlefield. From this view, it is possible to realize how small an area was involved, how close one was to one's enemy, and how personal war must have been. Return to your car and begin the Battlefield tour.

The Battlefield Tour

This time follow the RED arrow signs out of the car park (see Tour Map). The earthworks on the right are part of a line that surrounded the town and were meant to be, quite literally, city walls. They are not originals; the ones you see were built for the same reasons during the Civil War. Don't worry that you are hard pressed to locate the "horn-work" — it doesn't look like anything but another mound. It was an extension of the earthworks built out at an angle to provide extra defense for the road to Hampton. Your first stop is at the Grand battery, a reconstruction of the largest gun emplacement on the Allied line when the artillery opened fire on October 9, 1781. The bombardment was so successful that, two days later, Allied troops were able to open a second siege line — the point of your next stop. Both siege lines were trenches and gun emplacements; the first extended from the Grand Battery to the York River. The second had a couple of problems. It could not be extended all the way to the river because there were two snug English redoubts in the direct path. They (or rather reconstructions of them) are still there giving graphic focus to the tale of their taking. It is not easy to picture *several hundred* attackers and defenders in these oversized foxholes, but it is very easy to imagine being *one* of them. If one might be forgiven the pun, it is bloody easy.

Of course, the second siege line was completed after the redoubts were taken, and Cornwallis asked for terms after he failed to retake them and the Americans established a major artillery battery between the two. The silent cannons and mortars that stand there today are reproductions. As you go on to the next stop on the tour, Moore House, be aware that you are approaching the climax of the Revolutionary War. Here, in this altogether plain-looking little farmhouse, a great power gave up its claim to dictate ever again the fortunes of its American colonies.

Moore House

The tour of the house is conducted by interpreters from the National Park Service. Sometimes there is a wait of a few minutes before you can get in, but benches are provided in the pleasant little front yard over-looking the river. Inside, the house is a typical early Colonial farm-house with a narrow central hall between two wings, with square or rectangular rooms. The dining room, set with furnishings from the period, can be viewed only from the doorway. It is possible to view the kitchen and the bedrooms, but the real focal point is the "front parlor," where the negotiating teams met to arrange terms of surrender. Their words seem to hang in the air. Pick up the small Moore House brochure and read it on your way to the last stop, Surrender Field.

Climax

It's smaller than the paintings make it out to be. Take your place at
the stone terrace of the viewing tower and face the field. In a minute
the scene will be described to you (by the voice of actor William
Conrad), in stirring words and pictures, which, unlike so many record-
ings, enhance rather than detract. It's the high point in our story, seven
or eight generations removed from those three tiny ships that landed
just 15 miles away. Today's Americans are little more than seven or
eight generations removed from Yorktown.

Hard to believe, isn't it?

Amy Harald

THE COLONIAL PERIOD

Who, What, and When

by
ELEANOR AND JAMES LOUTTIT

The Fodor's Heritage Series is written to guide the traveler to and through the important, the intriguing, the beautiful, and the interesting places where the scenes of our history were played out. The editors feel there is a need for this type of guide to help those already in love with history and to perhaps lure others into the same love affair. This chapter of the guide includes background material that will put the people, places, and dates in perspective — the who, what, and when of America's brief Colonial period.

The biographies in this section have been chosen with care from a score or more that might have been included. The Royals are recorded here because, while we acknowledge our English roots, we don't always know much about them. Sir Walter Raleigh is here, for example, because it was his idea to start the whole emigration to the wilderness of the western colonies. George Washington is known to us all, but mostly for his great exploits rather than for his more mundane accomplishments. The others are included because they are interesting people germane to the story. The chronology of America's brief Colonial Period, which follows the biographical section, is a selection of the things that were happening in the world during the 175 years of our nation's minority.

The editors hope this chapter will add to your enjoyment and understanding of the Historic Triangle.

THE CAST

The Royals

Several monarchs occupied the throne of England during the 175 years before we became a nation. A few all but ignored their colonies amid the political maneuverings in their own bailiwick, and they are mentioned here only by name and dates to keep the record straight. Those half dozen who concerned themselves in some meaningful way with the Colonial period in America will be detailed.

Elizabeth I (1533–1603). She succeeded to the throne by virtue of outliving her royal siblings. Her young life was a revolving stage upon which she would be cast as a royal Princess one week, the next a royal bastard. The thought that her father (King Henry VIII) had ordered her mother (Anne Boleyn) to the headsman's ax was never far from her mind, and for all her days, after her coronation in 1558, she trusted no man. She knew that her only safety and that of her beloved realm lay in her controlling everything, from the purse strings to the succession. This she did with brilliant assurance in a glistening, exuberant time of history. She encouraged voyages to the New World, going so far as to give several of her sea captains "letters of marque" (commissions to patrol the seas for protection of British shipping), which in practice made them legal pirates. Their ventures filled her coffers as well as their own pockets. She was delighted to have stock companies attempt settlement of her far-off lands, but was not delighted enough to invest in them. Thus, Raleigh was coyly permitted to call the southern shores he explored "Virginia" in her honor and was pragmatically denied her financial backing. Owning things without having to pay for them was one of her talents.

Elizabeth was on her deathbed when she named the man who would succeed her — the son of her one-time second cousin and enemy, Mary, Queen of Scots — James VI of Scotland.

James I (1566–1625). Already King of Scotland (ruling as the sixth James), 37-year-old James Stuart became the first ruling monarch of the united kingdoms in 1603 when Elizabeth died. A strange little man, James I (and VI) suffered from porphyria — a debilitating liver disease — and was a chronic invalid. He was an unattractive man with a barrel-shaped body that his weak legs could barely support and a tongue, too large for his mouth, which caused him to drool. He was delighted to receive a new country from his cousin, because, whatever it was, it was richer than his own Scotland. Of that, he was certain.

James liked money but for different reasons from those of Elizabeth. She needed full coffers to ensure her being able to control everything; James wanted wealth to spend. Fortunately for England, he did not feel the need to prove his prowess in battle, and so his reign was peaceful. No, James spent his money on himself, his friends, his amusements, and even on his wife, Anne. His English subjects didn't like him very much; in fact, one, Guy Fawkes, tried to blow him (and Parliament) up. It was probably more from custom than from sincerity that the colonists named the first settlement Jamestown.

Among the accomplishments of James I were sponsorship of architect Inigo Jones's best works, the commissioning of the splendid King James version of the Bible, and the introduction of the game of golf. A most notable personal achievement: Unlike most of the other ruling members of his family, James died peacefully in bed.

Charles I (1600–1649). Kingship came to Charles by chance (his older brother Henry died in 1612), and it never quite seemed to fit him. He gave away (to eight of his best friends) a great chunk of the original Virginia and told them to call it "Carolana." The new owners didn't much care, ignored it as best they could, and thus almost ensured that for decades Jamestown would have no rival settlements to the south. Charles sometimes reminds us of the story of the Emperor's New Clothes, with his insistence that only God was his boss — a belief over which he, quite literally, lost his head.

Parliament ruled (1650–1653). After Charles I was executed, Parliament ruled during a period of stormy political turbulence.

Oliver Cromwell (1599–1658). Parliament surrendered power to Cromwell in 1653, and he became Lord Protector under a new constitution.

Richard Cromwell (1626–1712). The son of Oliver, he succeeded to the office of Lord Protector upon his father's death. Richard lacked the strength, talent, and support of the military that his father enjoyed. When he resigned under pressure from Parliament in 1659, turmoil resulted, and civil war loomed. A new Parliament proclaimed Charles II king in 1660.

Charles II (1630–1685). Reigned 1660 to 1685.

James II (1633–1701). Reigned 1685 to 1689.

William III and Mary II (1662–1694). The daughter and son-in-law of James II (they were both also grandchildren to Charles I), they already had a nice little country of their own — the Palatinate of Orange — across the channel, when they were invited to sit on the vacant throne of England in 1689. They were to rule jointly and equally, but — William being very bright, and Mary not, and William being a man, and Mary his wife — in fact, William ruled. When Mary died, the event was hardly noticed.

The pair ruled in what Churchill called "a queer, unnatural interlude," but they were immortalized in Williamsburg and the College of William and Mary. Mary's nephew, a favorite of William's, was the Duke of Gloucester, for whom the main street of Williamsburg was named.

Anne (1665–1714). Reigned 1702 to 1714.

George I (1660–1727). Reigned 1714 to 1727.

George II (1683–1760). Reigned 1727 to 1760.

George III (1738–1820). George's family was German (Hanoverian), and they never really became English. They let British ministers do the ruling, while they were either *in* Hanover or planning to *go* to Hanover. George III, however, recognized what power he could have just by exerting it in England.

The story of America might have been different if George hadn't expected so much. It upset him to find out that the colonists thought they had rights. He couldn't understand why they objected to what he thought was best for them — the Stamp Act, for example — and he took it as a personal affront. The whole uprising across the Atlantic seemed to him to be the tantrums of ungrateful children.

George suffered from porphyria, the family disease, as did James I, but after the loss at Yorktown, it manifested itself in psychosis. By 1810 George III was totally mad. He reigned 10 more years, but was "confined" during most of the excitement caused by Napoleon's campaigns across the Channel.

Nobility, Commoners, and Rebels

Sir Walter Raleigh (or Ralegh or Rawleyghe) (1554–1618). We first hear of Sir Walter as a Captain of the Guard, presumably the Palace Guard, at the court of Elizabeth I. A handsome, highly talented man, driven by ambition and willing to put on almost any face to further that ambition, Raleigh unabashedly flattered his way to the queen's side. She gave generously in return (of estates which did not lessen her purse, of course), and Raleigh gained position at court along with vast holdings in Ireland. The rivalry that grew between him and Robert Devereux, Earl of Essex, spurred him to foppery, poetry, and high adventure.

Walter Raleigh was a gentleman (knighted in 1584) who dressed in cloth-of-silver, and, as legend has it, gallantly laid his cloak over a puddle so his queen could cross unmuddied. He was a scholar who attended Oxford University, wrote philosophical and political theses, and set down poems with the best writers of his day. (He wrote the introductory sonnet to Spenser's "Faerie Queene.") He was a soldier-of-fortune who commanded an English army in Ireland, aided the French Huguenots in their wars against the Roman Catholic Church, and pirated Spanish merchant vessels in the New World. He was a businessman who financed a colonization company for two separate ventures, in an attempt to establish a settlement in the new lands he called "Virginia." Later in his career (1595), Raleigh made an expedition to South America and explored the Orinoco River in search of that ever-popular, but ever-elusive, El Dorado.

Raleigh fell out of Elizabeth's favor (as most everyone did at one time or another), but she forgave him after putting him in the Tower of London for a short stay. This was punishment for his marriage. (Elizabeth liked her courtiers to be devoted only to *her*.) After Elizabeth's death in 1603, the new king, James I, disinclined to trust those who had been favorites of his cousin the queen, charged Raleigh with treason, imprisoned him for 12 years, eventually released him, and finally, in 1616, executed him for "disobeying orders."

Among his other accomplishments, Sir Walter Raleigh is remembered for his popularizing the use of tobacco in England and for his introduction of the potato plant into Ireland.

John Smith (1580–1631). A plebian name for a man of many adventures, this John Smith was born in Lincolnshire, near the mouth of the Humber River in East Anglia. It's an amphibious land, full of great fens, big and small rivers, and the wash of the North Sea. Smith attended King Edward IV Grammar School in Louth before he became an apprentice to a local merchant, but he answered the call of the sea during England's period of naval superiority in the late 1500s. He fought the Spanish, attained his captaincy, learned soldiering as well as seamanship, and went off to fight the Turks in Hungary. There he was wounded, captured, and made a slave, then escaped and made his way across Europe to England. He was 26 years old when he sailed for Virginia with the men who would found Jamestown. There was trouble on the trip and, apparently, Smith was in the middle of it. He was accused of mutiny, but either because they needed every man or because the trouble was caused by good reason, Smith never had to answer any charges. His previous adventures and, possibly, his education made him eligible for the presiding council during the first critical year in the colony. His natural leadership ability (or his finally becoming fed up) made him take over management of the colony in late 1608. Its eventual success is directly attributable to his policies.

Smith explored almost the entire Chesapeake Bay before he was wounded in a gunpowder accident and forced to return to England in 1609. He returned to America in 1614, exploring the area around and north of Cape Cod. He named it "New England" and wrote a description of New England that the Pilgrims followed a few years later. He never realized his dream of founding a new colony in New England, but his later writings reveal that he saw the potential of the vast North American lands and visualized the nation that would emerge.

Francis Nicholson (1655–1728). He first appears in the history books when he is in his early thirties. We know nothing of his life before that, but we can make some very good guesses based on what he did *after* that. In 1688 Nicholson was serving as Lieutenant Governor of the New York Colony under Edmund Andros, who was then Royal Governor of "New England" (which included New York). Andros was on a trip to Boston when rebellion broke out in New York. Nicholson fled to England.

He came back in 1694 as Governor of Maryland Province at the new capital city, Annapolis. He designed most of the town and watched it become a major commercial center during his four-year tenure. His transfer to the Governorship of the Virginia Colony (1698) was not necessarily a step up because he wrote in a report in 1701, "Formerly there was good convenient land to be taken up, and there were widows had pretty good fortunes, which were encouragement for men of parts to come. But now all or most of these good lands are taken up, and if there be any widows or maids of any fortune, the Natives for the most part get them; for they begun to have a sort of aversion to others, calling them strangers." Could the Governor have been looking for a wife? — or a fortune?

Nicholson laid out the city of Williamsburg but took time from his labors to declare an annual field day in 1701, limiting contestants to "the better sort of Virginians." But something went wrong while he was governor, because in 1704 he wrote "A Modest Answer to a Malicious Libel" in defense of his own conduct, and in 1705 he was no longer in Virginia. He turned up next in 1711 as a colonel and helped capture Port Royal in Nova Scotia and was named Governor of that province by Queen Anne. When she died in 1713, he dropped from sight once again. Seven years later, he became Governor of South Carolina, where he served for five years.

A good history sleuth might conclude that Nicholson was an educated younger son of well-to-do parents, dependent upon political connections, and somewhat of a snob. The bounces in his career and his (comparative) old age at death label him a survivor.

The Warriors

Charles Cornwallis (First Marquis Cornwallis) (1738–1805). At age 16, Eton-educated Charles Cornwallis was commissioned an ensign (junior officer rank) in the British army. He saw service in Europe during the Seven Years War (French and Indian War in America), entered politics about 10 years later, and was on hand in Parliament to oppose some of the taxation acts that led to the American Revolution. He swallowed the "I-told-you-so," followed tradition and entered military service again to fight the rebellious Americans. He acquitted himself with honor while serving under Generals Howe and Clinton in several engagements. Most of his campaigns were successes, but he is remembered in America for his monumental failure — defeat and surrender at Yorktown.

Apparently his explanation of that disaster was satisfactory to the powers-that-were, because, five years later, Cornwallis was appointed Governor General of India. When he arrived in Calcutta, "a sink of corruption and iniquity," he found he had inherited a "system of the dirtiest jobbery." He proceeded to initiate revolutionary reforms while believing that every Indian was corrupt to his marrow, and he wasn't too sure about some of the British either. He joined the military campaign in Mysore and, in general, did such a good job that he was called home in 1794 to become Viceroy to Ireland.

That didn't turn out to be a perfect plum of a reward. Cornwallis didn't bring on the Irish Rebellion of 1798, but he swiftly and oppressively put it down. His was the plan for uniting Ireland and England in the unhappy Act of Union in 1800. Apparently, he was relieved (with honors) from his post in Ireland shortly thereafter, since we next find him engaged in drawing up the Treaty of Amiens, which halted (briefly) the Napoleonic Wars.

In 1805 it was back to India, where there was a heap of trouble. He set out with an army up the Ganges to suppress the revolt, but he died and was buried on the way at Ghazipur. A statue of Cornwallis, dressed in a toga(!), stands today in the Victoria Memorial at Calcutta.

George Washington (1732–1799). Born to Augustus (Gus) and Mary Ball Washington, the eldest of their six children, George was to become a "father" himself some 50 years later — the father of his country. Gus Washington had four children by his first wife, and the oldest of that group was George's idol. When George was 11, Gus died and the idol, Lawrence, became surrogate father. The family was well-to-do, and Lawrence added to their fortune by marrying into the Fairfax family. George's formal education had been meager but, when he was 15, Colonel Fairfax invited him to accompany a surveying party to the Fairfax holdings west of the Blue Ridge. Two years later, George was made official surveyor of Culpeper County, his first public office. If he didn't cut down the famous cherry tree, he certainly did cut down a lot of other trees in *that* job.

While on a trip to Barbados with Lawrence in 1752, George contracted smallpox and survived, thus ensuring his own immunity against the scourge that would later run through his army. When Lawrence died in 1752, George inherited part of his estate as well as some of his duties as county adjutant. Thus he became Major Washington and was in charge of training militia. He was an ambitious young man who volunteered for things, one of those things being to carry a warning to the French in the Ohio Territory (1753) that they were trespassing on British lands. While he was with the French, he learned that they were planning to go on to Fort Duquesne (later Fort Pitt, then Pittsburgh). Washington hurried home with the news, was made a lieutenant-colonel, and was given a troop of militia to take back to the Ohio Territory and prevent the French advance. He was too late to save Duquesne, but he won his first battle at a hastily built camp post (Fort Necessity) and was made a colonel.

When the French recovered from the surprise of being defeated by such a puny force, they roundly beat him in the next battle. Colonel Washington was General Braddock's aide when Braddock made a great mess of trying to recapture Fort Duquesne in 1755. Washington was made Commander-in-Chief of the Virginia militia and was with General Forbes when the British finally occupied the now-abandoned Fort Duquesne.

When his military career ended (temporarily), George concentrated on his personal life. It was reported (probably gossiped about, too) that he was in love with his neighbor's wife, but he married a rich widow,

Martha Custis, instead. They settled down to a long, prosperous, and happy married life at Mount Vernon, Virginia. The military craft Washington learned as a young man in the western territories served him well, if not completely, when he was named Commander-in-Chief of the Continental Army. He made several blunders that a career general probably wouldn't have made, but his strength of character and personality were his saving graces. He was an amiable man but so strongly moral and just that he appeared cold. He was obstinate and lacked humor, but he was extremely sensitive. He was rich and acquisitive, but he never deserted his ragged, hungry men at Valley Forge. He was a leader because he believed himself to be one, and other men believed it, too.

Washington died after his terms as President "first in war, first in peace, and first in the hearts of his countrymen." His memorials are too numerous to be listed here, but some notable ones are his home at Mount Vernon, the Monument obelisk in the nation's capital, countless statues (including one in the Smithsonian Institute that portrays him wearing a toga), and, unbelievable as it may seem, one in front of the National Gallery in London. There's also a national holiday, a preserved homestead in Sulgrave Manor, England (the family estate for over 120 years), and the millions of apple trees around Winchester, Virginia, where Washington once owned land and required his tenants to plant four apple trees on each acre.

THE STAGE

A Chronology of America's Brief Colonial Period

1607–1781

Bronze-skinned nomads from eastern Asia had "colonized" parts of the North American continent as long as 20,000 years before, but, for our purpose here, "America's Brief Colonial Period" is little more than a few short footnotes in human history.

And brief it was — a mere 174 years between the founding of the first *permanent* English settlement at Jamestown in the spring of 1607 and the humiliation of a haughty British army at Yorktown in the fall of 1781.

Indian deerhunters drifted eastward to Chesapeake Bay as early as 8000 B.C. Some liked what they found and stayed. Descendants of these first black-haired, dark-eyed Stone Age travelers later became the Powhatan Confederacy, a scattered group of some 30 Eastern Woodland tribes whose loose "family" tie was the Algonquin language. The Powhatan, when the first English settlers arrived, were comfortably ensconced in some 200 palisaded villages along coastal Virginia and around the shores of Chesapeake Bay. Like their Stone Age ancestors, they hunted rabbits and deer in the woodlands, but they also raised corn and enjoyed the fish, crabs, and oysters of the bountiful bay.

We also know that Viking wanderers touched America's eastern shores as early as A.D. 1000 and that Columbus sailed westward from Spain in 1492 and "discovered" North America. For the next few centuries, Spanish soldiers, priests, and adventurers busied themselves in South and Central America (and even Florida, Texas, New Mexico, and California), converting the natives and looking for gold. Spaniards visited the Chesapeake in the early 1500s, and Giovanni de Verrazano, sailing for France, probably sailed into the bay in 1524, but the bay remained relatively peaceful through most of that century. Although English seadogs like Drake, Gilbert, and Raleigh were harassing Spanish shipping in the Americas, the British Crown gave little serious thought to New World colonization until her captains had smashed the Spanish Armada in 1588.

The first attempt by Englishmen to settle in the New World was made in 1585, when Sir Walter dispatched a small band of settlers westward across the Atlantic. Those first English colonists landed on Roanoke Island, between North Carolina's Albemarle and Pamlico Sounds. They sailed home to England in 1586. A second group tried again in the same place the following year, but they disappeared without a trace by the time the busy folks back home finally got around to sending them supplies in 1591. That second desperate little band has gone down in history as The Lost Colony of Roanoke.

True to character, the British tried again, this time landing further north at Jamestown, near the entrance to the great bay. The date was May 14, 1607 — Year One of the following chronology.

1608

This was the "starveing tyme" for the struggling Virginia Colony. Captain John Smith emerged as the colony's strongman, but also found time to explore the great bay to the north.

1609

This was the last year of the new colony's "starveing tyme." Life was anything but easy, but the settlers were beginning to move inland, away from the marshy shores. Further north, Henry Hudson sailed into New York harbor and explored the lush river area that came to be known as the Hudson River Valley. Still further north, Samuel de Champlain explored the land around Lake Champlain, named in his honor.

1610

Baron Thomas West de la Warr arrived from England and persuaded Jamestown's surviving colonists to hang on, and surprisingly, they did. Busy Explorer Hudson, who would die the following year, discovered and explored the bay area, later named Hudson Bay.

1612

John Smith, who was no longer with the colony at Jamestown, published "A Map of Virginia." At Jamestown, John Rolfe began to cultivate tobacco, helping to insure the colony's survival.

1613

Jamestown colonists crossed native tobacco with a West Indian leaf and produced a variety that soon became the rage in England.

1614

Rolfe married Pocahontas, the Powhatan "princess" who had saved John Smith from her irate father some years before.

1615

Back in England, Smith published *A Description of New England.*

1619

The House of Burgesses, the first representative assembly in the New World, was elected at Jamestown. The first black indentured servants were brought to America that year by Dutch traders at Jamestown.

1620

The Virginia Company now held a monopoly on tobacco sales in England. Further up the coast, in what would be called Massachusetts, Puritan separatists from the Church of England missed Virginia and landed on December 21 on the *Mayflower* at Plymouth, where they signed the "Mayflower Compact." Half the colonists died the following winter, among them John Carver, the Plymouth Colony's first governor.

1621

The Dutch West India Company was formed. It later claimed the coast from Chesapeake Bay north to Newfoundland.

1624

The Dutch ship, *New Netherland,* left eight crewmen on Manhattan Island (New York Harbor) and sailed upriver as far as the future city of Albany.

1626

Peter Minuit purchased Manhattan Island from local Indians for $24 worth of trinkets. In England, the prolific John Smith published *A General History of Virginia, New England, and the Summer Isles.* In New England, Roger Conant settled Salem.

1631

The Dutch West India Company established a settlement on Delaware Bay.

1632

Charles I issued a charter to Lord Baltimore for the Maryland Colony.

1633

The Dutch settled in Connecticut.

1634

Maryland colonists aboard the *Arc* and the *Dove* landed at the mouth of the Potomac River to found a Catholic colony based on religious tolerance.

1635

A secondary school, the first in North America, was founded in Boston.

1636

Compulsory education was established in Boston, and Harvard College was founded at Newe Towne, Cambridge, Massachusetts. Also in New England, Roger Williams founded a "democratic colony" at the future Providence, Rhode Island.

1644

A charter was granted to the Providence colony in the future Rhode Island.

1649

Puritan exiles from Virginia settled in Providence, Maryland.

1650

Chattel slavery was legally recognized in the colonies. In Boston, Harvard College was granted its charter.

1660

In England, Parliament passed the Navigation Act, which severely regulated Colonial commerce and marked the first of future squabbles between the colonists and the government of their former homeland.

1664

Peter Stuyvesant surrendered New Amsterdam to British troops, and it was renamed New York. Fort Orange, up the Hudson, was renamed Albany.

1665

English law and administration were introduced in New York, and the Colony of New Jersey was founded.

1666

Connecticut Puritans settled in Newark, New Jersey.

1669

John Locke's Carolina Constitution was approved, and South Carolina was founded.

1670

Charleston, South Carolina, was founded as Charles Towne.

1674

The Treaty of Westminster (England) recognized the citizens of New York as British subjects.

1676

Nathaniel Bacon led a revolt against British Governor Berkeley of Virginia, and Jamestown was burned. Bacon died, and 23 rebels were executed. "King" Philip Wampanoag, chief of the Narragansetts, was killed, ending the bloody Indian wars in New England.

1677

Massachusetts bought part of Maine from the heirs of Sir Ferdinando Gorges.

1678

Thomas Thatcher's *A Brief Rule in Small Pocks or Measles* was the first medical treatise published in America.

1679

New Hampshire separated as a "special province" from Massachusetts.

1683

William Penn signed a treaty with the Delaware Indians and made payment for land in Pennsylvania. Penn also published "A General Description of Pennsylvania."

1684

England annulled Massachusetts's charter.

1689

William and Mary recognized old Colonial charters.

1690

The first Colonial newspaper, *Publick Occurrences,* was suppressed after its first publication in Boston.

1691

Massachusetts absorbed Plymouth Colony and was granted a new charter.

1692

Nineteen "witches" were put to death in Danvers (then Salem, Massachusetts). William and Mary College was founded in Williamsburg, Virginia.

1696

American Captain Kidd turned pirate. Five years later he was arrested and hanged in England.

1701

The Collegiate School chartered in Saybrook, Connecticut (to become Yale University).

1703

Delaware separated from Pennsylvania and became a colony.

1704

Indians attacked Deerfield, Massachusetts, killing 40 settlers and abducting 100 others. *Boston News Letter,* the first successful Colonial newspaper, was published.

1707

Back home, England and Scotland were united as Great Britain.

1711

Indians massacred 200 North Carolina settlers during the Tuscarora War.

1712

Twenty-one black slaves were executed during an uprising in New York. Thirty years later, 26 more were executed and 71 deported after another revolt, also in New York.

1716

The first Colonial theater was opened in Williamsburg. The Collegiate School moved from Saybrook, Connecticut, to New Haven.

1718

The Collegiate School became known as Yale College. (The name Yale University was adopted in 1887.)

1720

William Burnet, Governor of New York, extended trade with the Indians.

1722

Samuel Adams, the American revolutionary, was born in Boston.

1728

The *Pennsylvania Gazette* was founded in Philadelphia. Benjamin Franklin bought an interest in the paper the following year.

1729

North and South Carolina became British Crown Colonies.

1732

Benjamin Franklin's *Poor Richard's Almanack* was issued in the colonies. George Washington was born in Virginia.

1733

James Oglethorpe founded Savannah, Georgia.

1734

The first formal horse race in America was held in Charleston Neck, South Carolina.

1735

New York recognized freedom of the press by acquitting John Peter Zenger, of the *Weekly Journal,* of a libel charge against the British governor.

1736

Patrick Henry, the American revolutionary, was born in Virginia.

1738

British troops were sent to Georgia to settle a Florida/Georgia border dispute with Spain.

1739

George Clinton, who would twice become a U.S. vice president, was born in New York. Also that year, an American astronomer, John Winthrop IV, published *Notes on Sunspots.*

1740

The University of Pennsylvania was founded.

1742

Nathaniel Greene, the American revolutionary general, was born in Rhode Island.

1744

Date of the King George's War — British and American colonials against the French and the Indians, known in Europe as the Seven Years War. Colonials captured Louisburg on Cape Breton Island, which was returned to France the following year.

1746

The College of New Jersey, later known as Princeton, was founded.

1747

John Paul Jones, the American naval officer, was born in Scotland.

1749

The Philadelphia Academy, later the University of Pennsylvania, was founded.

1750

Henry Knox, the American revolutionary leader, was born in Boston.

1752

Benjamin Franklin flew his kite and discovered the electric conductor.

1754

King's College, later Columbia University, was founded in New York. In the west, the third French and Indian War began when the French occupied Fort Duquesne (later Pittsburgh). The French gave up Canada and the American midwest when peace was negotiated in 1763. During this time, the Crown tightened the reins on its rambunctious American colonies.

1755

Alexander Hamilton, the American revolutionary and statesman, was born in the West Indies.

1756

Aaron Burr, the American statesman who would later kill Hamilton in a duel, was born in New Jersey.

1758

George Washington and John Forbes recaptured Fort Duquesne from the French.

1763

A British proclamation provided governments for Florida and Quebec, Canada.

1764

Britain amended the Sugar Act to tax her American colonies. Duties were also imposed on lumber, molasses, and rum.

1765

Britain passed the Stamp Act, taxing her American subjects to help support royal troops in those colonies. The Virginia Assembly challenged the tax, and nine colonies, led by New York and Pennsylvania, adopted, at a Stamp Act Congress, a declaration that "taxation without representation" was tyranny.

1766

Britain repealed the Stamp Act, but reasserted her right to tax the colonies. That same year Mason and Dixon surveyed the boundary between Pennsylvania (north) and Maryland (south).

1767

Britain taxed tea, glass, pepper, and dyestuffs in the colonies, causing an uproar in Boston. Most of these Townshend Act duties (except for tea) were repealed three years later. That year, the New York Assembly was suspended for refusing to quarter British troops.

1768

Boston refused to quarter British troops.

1769

The Virginia Assembly was dissolved after protesting British treason trials of American colonials.

1770

British troops fired on a Boston mob, killing five persons.

1772

The Boston Assembly, advocating the rights of the colonists, threatened secession. Samuel Adams formed the Committees of Correspondence in Massachusetts for action against Great Britain.

1773

The Virginia House of Burgesses appointed a Provincial Committee of Correspondence. That same year, an East India tea ship was burned at Annapolis, and on December 16, Boston dumped a cargo of tea into the harbor — the Boston Tea Party.

1774

"Intolerable Acts" of British Parliament curtailed self-rule in Massachusetts and barred further use of the harbor until Bostonians repaid the cost of all that soggy tea. The Virginia House of Commons called the Continental Congress, which met in Philadelphia, with representatives from all the colonies except Georgia. The Congress resolved to restrict importation of British goods and called for "civil disobedience." That year, Rhode Island abolished slavery.

1775

Patrick Henry, addressing the Virginia convention, proclaimed, "Give me liberty or give me death." Paul Revere and William Dawes rode through the Massachusetts countryside on April 18 to alert patriots that British troops were marching on Concord to destroy a store of American arms. The next day, at Lexington, eight Colonial militiamen were killed, but the British suffered 273 casualties returning from Concord. In May, colonels Ethan Allen and Benedict Arnold captured Fort Ticonderoga in New York from the British, and in early June Americans twice repulsed British troops on Breed's Hill — the Battle of Bunker Hill — before giving ground. British troops suffered 1,000 casualties. In mid-June, the Continental Congress in Philadelphia named George Washington Commander-in-Chief of the fledgling American Army. After his success at Fort Ticonderoga, Arnold's attack on Quebec, Canada, failed. In Europe, England hired 29,000 German mercenaries to help put down the growing revolt in her North American colonies.

1776

France and Spain agreed in the spring to help arm the Americans against their traditional foe, England. In June, in the Continental Congress, Richard Henry Lee of Virginia moved "that these united colonies are and of right ought to be free and independent states." The resolution was adopted on July 2, and the Declaration of Independence was approved two days later. Congress then retired to Baltimore. In the north, Arnold's Lake Champlain fleet was defeated at Valcour, but Washington forced the British out of Boston. In the middle colonies, Washington, with 10,000 men, lost the battle of Long Island and evacuated New York in August. The British, commanded by General William Howe, failed to destroy Washington's army at White Plains in New York, but captured 3,000 men at Fort Washington in Manhattan on November 16, and two days later captured Fort Lee on the opposite bank of the Hudson River. Earlier, on June 28, in the south, American batteries at Charleston, South Carolina, had repulsed a British naval attack. Near the close of the year, on Christmas night, Washington's forces crossed the Delaware River from Pennsylvania and defeated 1,400 Hessians at Trenton, New Jersey, on December 26. During this momentous year, Nathan Hale ("I only regret that I have but one life to lose for my country") was hanged as a spy by the British without trial.

1777

This was a year of ups and downs for the American cause. It opened with Washington's victory over General Lord Cornwallis at Princeton, New Jersey, and it closed with Washington's cold and hungry troops in winter quarters at Valley Forge, Pennsylvania. During that year, American forces won at Bennington, Vermont, but lost at Brandywine and Germantown in Pennsylvania, and the British gained control of Delaware. Further north, British General John Burgoyne, commanding an army of 8,000 men from Canada, recaptured Fort Ticonderoga, but lost two battles at Bemis Heights and surrendered 5,000 soldiers at Saratoga, New York, in October. Also during the year, the first French troops, commanded by the 20-year-old Marquis de Lafayette, arrived in America, as did German General von Steuben, who became Inspector-General of Washington's army. The Continental Congress adopted the Articles of Confederation and Perpetual Union, and chose the Stars and Stripes as the country's flag. In the closing days of that year, France, America's ally, recognized the independence of Britain's 13 North American colonies.

1778

Early in the year, France and Holland signed treaties with the Americans, and France sent a fleet to America, forcing the British to evacuate Philadelphia. Washington defeated British forces at Monmouth, New Jersey, but the British captured Savannah, Georgia, in the south. England's allies, the Indians, massacred Americans at Wyoming, Pennsylvania and Cherry Valley in New York during the year, and the colonies rejected a peace offer from the mother country.

1779

Congress dispatched a force against the Indians in the Wyoming Valley (see 1778), and American forces won a victory at Vincennes (now Indiana) against British troops. In Europe, John Paul Jones, aboard the *Bonhomme Richard,* defeated the British *Serapis* in the North Sea.

1780

With the focus of the war now in the south, the British captured Charleston, South Carolina, and refused to recognize the defeated Americans as the army of a sovereign nation. Americans were also defeated at Camden, South Carolina, but Colonial militiamen won a victory over British troops at King's Mountain, South Carolina. In the north, more French troops arrived at Newport, Rhode Island. Benedict Arnold's plot to surrender West Point, in New York, to the British was revealed, but Arnold escaped and became a British general.

American continentals and militiamen defeated the British at Cowpens and Eutaw, South Carolina, then lost at Guilford Courthouse in North Carolina. From there General Cornwallis withdrew his depleted army to Wilmington, North Carolina, on the coast and moved north to Virginia to set the stage for the climactic Battle of Yorktown and the surrender of the British army on October 19.

As far as active campaigning was concerned, Yorktown ended the war. Although the British and Americans held their positions near New York and Charleston for nearly two more years, the only fighting was some minor skirmishing in the south. America's brief Colonial period ended on a dusty field just outside Yorktown, Virginia, and England faced the reality of the end in March of 1782, when a new British cabinet recognized the independence of her former North American colonies. A formal treaty between Great Britain and the United States of America was signed at Versailles, France, the following year, and George Washington disbanded his victorious Continental Army.

PRACTICAL
INFORMATION

THE HISTORIC TRIANGLE

Introductory Information

Compiled by
JAMES LOUTTIT

It's a small stage, and there are only three principal players. There are bit players by the score, of course, and a supporting cast that numbers in the many thousands, but Jamestown, Williamsburg, and Yorktown are always center stage, and that is why this historic trio is so wonderfully unique.

Situated in a lop-sided triangle that is scarcely more than a dozen crow-flying miles across its base, the three sites are tied together by the gently curving Colonial Parkway — an easy and pleasant drive from any one site to each of the others.

The path of history has many forks and turns, but there is a certain logic as to why these three historic gems are located here — and why they should be explored as a unit. None, in its beginning, was located more than a long day's march from its nearest neighbor, and this proximity serves us well today. Any one of the three is worth a separate visit, but the *total* experience is far greater than the sum of the three separate parts.

If our writers and editors have fulfilled their mission, they have whetted your appetite to savor the Jamestown, Williamsburg, and Yorktown Story as a trilogy — the beginning, middle, and end of America's Colonial Experience. That Story and our present-day guide to the Experience were presented in the preceding chapters. The following chapters contain comprehensive listings of Places to Stay, Places to Eat, and Things to See and Do — selections that hopefully will ease your way as you travel back through some 38 decades to this brief segment in America's heritage, the 175-year period between the landing at Jamestown in 1607 and the climactic battle at Yorktown in 1781.

Note finally that the following three major chapters, PLACES TO STAY, PLACES TO EAT, and THINGS TO SEE AND DO, have been subdivided, where appropriate, for easy reference into nine separate historic or geographic sections:

- Jamestown
- Colonial Williamsburg
- Merchants Square
- Along Richmond Road
- In and Around Williamsburg
- Northwest of Williamsburg
- Yorktown
- Hampton
- Newport News

Amy Harold

PLACES TO STAY

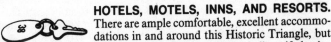

HOTELS, MOTELS, INNS, AND RESORTS.
There are ample comfortable, excellent accommodations in and around this Historic Triangle, but visitors may find that hard to believe if they've neglected to book ahead during the peak summer touring season. Reserve well in advance, and you should have no problem finding suitable accommodations within an easy drive of Jamestown, Williamsburg, and Yorktown, or the other attractions on the peninsula between the York and James rivers. Although space limitations restrict the length of the following lists, we have attempted to provide a comprehensive and representative *selection,* keeping convenience, personal tastes, and the traveler's pocketbook always in mind. Our categories follow the same general price ranges throughout: *Deluxe,* $100 and up; *Expensive,*

$75–$100; *Moderate,* $40–$75; and *Inexpensive,* under $40. All are based on double occupancy.

Jamestown

Although there are no accommodations in or immediately adjacent to the Jamestown Colonial National Historical Park, Williamsburg is only a few miles away, and Yorktown is just a bit farther. It might be worth mentioning here that Williamsburg, at the apex of the Historic Triangle, is less than 40 miles northwest of Norfolk (via I–64 or U.S. 60), and the distance from Newport News or Hampton, both at the southern end of the Virginia Peninsula, is even shorter. For a selection of accommodations, restaurants, and attractions in the Norfolk area, see either *Fodor's Virginia* or *Fodor's Chesapeake* travel guides. Accommodations at the lower end of the Peninsula are listed later in this guide.

Colonial Williamsburg

The first six listings in the following selections are operated by the Colonial Williamsburg Foundation and are located within or immediately adjacent to the Historic Area. Reservations or further information may be obtained for each of these six foundation listings by contacting Reservation Manager, Colonial Williamsburg Foundation, Box B, Williamsburg, VA 23187; 229–1000 or 800–HISTORY. Foundation accommodations require a deposit of $75 to hold a reservation. AE, MC, V accepted.

Williamsburg Inn. *Deluxe.* Off Francis St., Colonial Williamsburg; address and telephone numbers above. A distinguished hotel in a stately setting, the Inn's Regency-furnished lobby, lounges, and guest rooms capture the sedate luxury of a Virginia country estate. There are 151 rooms in the Inn, with an additional 85 guest rooms in 26 Colonial houses and 43 more in the Inn's contemporary wings (see below).

White Lion Motel. *Inexpensive.* 912 Capitol Landing Rd.; 229–3931. 38 units, 18 with kitchens. 1 mile from Historic Area. AE, MC, V.

Williamsburg Hilton & Conference Center. *Expensive to Deluxe.* 50 Kingsmill Rd.; 2 ½ miles east on U.S. 60; 220–2500. 300 rooms, some units with private patios and balconies. Restaurants, bar, room service, and pool. Adjacent to Busch Gardens. All major credit cards.

Yorktown Inn of Williamsburg. *Moderate.* 7135 Pocahantas Trail, midway between Colonial Williamsburg and Busch Gardens; 229–6900 or (800) 841–9100. 100 rooms, including suites with wet bar and refrigerators. Sammy & Nick's Steak House (229–3717). Underground parking. All major credit cards.

Northwest of Williamsburg

Anderson's Motel. *Inexpensive to Moderate.* 8550 Richmond Rd., near I–64, U.S. 60, Toano 23168; 566–0032. 14 rooms. MC, V.

Best Western Williamsburg Outlet. *Moderate.* U.S. 60 at Rte. 646 or Box 3108, Lightfoot 23187; 565–1000. 193 rooms, adjacent to Outlets Ltd. Mall and ⅛ mile from Pottery Factory. Indoor pool, lounge. All major credit cards.

Passport Inn. *Moderate.* 6488 Richmond Rd. or Box 528, Lightfoot 23090; 565–0090 or (800) 238–6161. 73 rooms, within walking distance of Pottery and Outlets Ltd. Mall. All major credit cards.

Yorktown

Visitors to the Historic Triangle tend to base themselves in or close to Williamsburg, where there is a wide selection of accommodations in all price ranges, or in Newport News or Hampton (see below), both seldom more than a half-hour's drive from most Virginia Peninsula attractions. The following are a few "local" Yorktown accommodations:

Duke of York. *Moderate.* Water St., on Rte. 238, 1 block east of the bridge; 898–3232. 57 rooms with balconies. Restaurant. Opposite a beach, overlooking the York River. MC, V.

Thomas Nelson Motel. *Moderate.* 2501 George Washington Hwy., U.S. 17, 3 miles south of Yorktown; 898–5436. 26 units with kitchenette. Pool.

Tidewater Motel. *Moderate.* 4 miles north of Yorktown (over the bridge, U.S. 17); 642–2155 or 642–6604. 33 rooms. Pool. Restaurants nearby. Picnic area.

Yorktown Motor Lodge. *Inexpensive.* 3 ½ miles south of bridge on U.S. 17; 898–5451. 52 rooms, some with private patios.

Hampton

Econo Lodge. *Inexpensive.* 2708 W. Mercury Blvd., Hampton 23666; 826–8970 or (800) 446–6900. 72 rooms. AE, DC, MC, V.

Hampton Inn. *Inexpensive to Moderate.* 1813 Mercury Blvd., Hampton 23666; 838–8484 or (800) HAMPTON. 132 rooms. Pool. AE, CB, DC, MC, V.

Holiday Inn — Coliseum. *Moderate.* 1815 W. Mercury Blvd., Hampton 23666; Jct. I–64 and U.S. 258; 838–0200 or (800) HOLIDAY. 275 rooms in two-story inn. Pool, bar, and room service. Some suites and meeting rooms. AE, MC, V.

La Quinta Motor Inn. *Moderate.* 2138 W. Mercury Blvd., Hampton 23666; 827–8680 or (800) 531–5900. 130 rooms, with restaurant and pool. AE, CB, DC, MC, V.

Sheraton Inn-Coliseum. *Moderate to Expensive.* 1215 W. Mercury Blvd., Hampton 23666; 838–5011 or (800) 325–3535. Newly renovated, with restaurant, lounge, and indoor pool. 187 rooms, with a concierge floor. AE, CB, DC, MC, V.

Strawberry Banks Motor Inn. *Moderate.* 30 Strawberry Banks Ln., Hampton 23666; 723–6061 or (800) 446–4088. 104 rooms, convenient location near Exit 69, I–64. Restaurant and pool. AE, CB, DC, MC, V.

Newport News

Econo Lodge. *Inexpensive to Moderate.* 15237 Warwick Blvd., Newport News 23606; 874–9244. 47 rooms. AE, MC, V.

Holiday Inn. *Moderate.* 6128 Jefferson Ave., Newport News 23605; 826–4500 or (800) HOLIDAY. 162 rooms in a five-story motor inn. Restaurant, bar, and room service. Major credit cards.

Olde London Inn. *Moderate.* 11003 Jefferson Ave., Newport News 23601; 599–6193. 130 rooms. Pool. AE, DC, MC, V.

Ramada Inn. *Moderate.* 950 J. Clyde Morris Blvd., Newport News 23601; Jct. Rte. 17 and I–64; 599–4460 or (800) 2RAMADA. 164 rooms, with 24-hour restaurant and lighted tennis courts. All major credit cards.

Thr-rift Inn South. *Inexpensive.* 6129 Jefferson Ave., Newport News 23605; 877–6251 or (800) 446–1066. 102 rooms, some with refrigerators. AE, MC, V.

Traveler's Inn. *Inexpensive.* 14747 Warwick Blvd., Newport News 23602; U.S. 60; 874–0201. 118 rooms. Restaurant. AE, DC, CB, MC, V.

Warwick Motel. *Inexpensive.* 12304 Warwick Blvd., Newport News 23606, Rte. 60 at J. Clyde Morris Blvd.; 599–4444. 31 rooms. Restaurant. AE, MC, V.

 CAMPING. In tune with the times, there are a number of convenient, multiple-facility "camping grounds" in and around the Historic Triangle, catering to the needs of the trailer, RV, and tenting public. Most, as you know, have minimum-age requirements, others do not allow pets, and still others offer specialized services for additional fees. The wise camper plans well ahead, both to reserve a space and check the facilities. In general, the rates per site range from $6 to $12 for two to four persons. Here are a few Williamsburg sites, with their locations, phone numbers, restriction exceptions, and operating schedules:

Anvil Campgrounds. 60 sites. 3 miles northwest of Colonial Williamsburg, U.S. 60W, Box 1774, Williamsburg 23185; 565–2300. Open all year.

Brass Lantern Campground. 40 sites. 1782 Jamestown Rd., Rte. 31, between Jamestown and Williamsburg; 229–4320 or 229–9089. No minimum-age requirements. Open all year.

Colonial Campgrounds — Safari. 200 sites. Rte. 4, Box 341C; Rte. 646, off I–64 north of Williamsburg; 565–2734 or (800) 251–9740. Open all year.

Fair Oaks Best Holiday Trav-L-Park. 300 sites. Rte. 9, Box 294-A; Rte. 646 via U.S. 60 or I-64; 565–2101. Open all year.

First Settlers' Campground. 200 sites. Box BE, Rte. 31S and James-town Rd., south of Rte. 199; 229–4900. Open April through November.

Five Forks Campsites. 60 sites. Rte. 3, Box 243; 3 miles west on Rte. 5; 229–5026. No minimum-age requirements. Open all year.

Ft. Cherokee Campground & Trading Post. 30 sites. 8758 Pocahantas Trail, U.S. 60, across from Carter's Grove; 220–0386. Open all year.

Indian Village Campground. 95 sites. 1811 Jamestown Rd.; Rte. 31, southeast of Rte. 199; 229–8211. Open all year.

Jamestown Beach Campsites. 600 sites. Box CB; 3 ½ miles south on Rte. 31 and James River; 229–7609 or 229–3300. Open all year.

Kin-Kaid Kampground. 50 sites. 599 Rochambeau Dr., Rte. 646 and Lightfoot Exit off I-64, east ¼ mile; 565–2010. No minimum-age requirements. Open mid-March through mid-November.

Williamsburg Campsites Inc. 300 sites. Rte. 9, Box 274; 4 ½ miles west on U.S. 60; 564–3101. No minimum-age requirements. Open all year.

Williamsburg "KOA." 100 sites. Rte. 4, Box 340B; 5 miles northeast on Rte. 646 via U.S. 60; 565–2907. Open March 1 to December 6.

PLACES TO EAT

**RESTAURANTS, TAVERNS, GRILLS, AND CAFETERIAS.** Eating out is an integral part of the travel experience. Always a necessity, often a pleasure, and sometimes a delight, dining out should never be a chore and certainly not a disaster. Planning ahead — matching your mood, appetite, and wallet to a particular restaurant — can spell the difference between eating for sustenance and dining for pleasure. If nothing else, eating out should be a relaxing break in your busy schedule — a time to plan the day ahead or review the day just past. And, above all, eating out should rarely be a catch-as-catch-can affair, which is why this section of our guide is as comprehensive as space permits. There is no shortage of excellent places to eat in and around the Historic Triangle, and the following selections are far from

all-inclusive. If you discover a very special place that the editors have overlooked, we'd be delighted to hear about it. As in our Places to Stay section, our selections lead off with those establishments that are operated by the Colonial Williamsburg Foundation, primarily because they are located within or adjacent to the Historic Area. Except for the Motor House Cafeteria and the Clubhouse Grill, reservations are usually a must at most, if not all, Historic Area restaurants. Reservations are also recommended for many other fine restaurants throughout the area. As a general rule, the categories below are based on the dinner cost per person, excluding wine, cocktails, and tip. They are: *Deluxe*, $25 or more; *Expensive*, $15–$25; *Moderate*, $7–$15; and *Inexpensive*, under $7. Lunch, of course, is usually considerably less expensive than dinner. And one final note: Although there is an indoor-outdoor cafeteria and picnic area at Jamestown Festival Park, this historic site has no fine restaurants for evening dining.

Colonial Williamsburg Taverns

Josiah Chowning's Tavern. *Expensive.* On Market Square, corner of Queen and Duke of Gloucester sts. in the Historic Area; 229–2141. Traditional good food and nightly entertainment starting at 9 P.M. in a reconstructed 18th-century alehouse. Lunch and dinner outdoors, weather permitting. Brunswick stew and prime beef are specialties. Lunch (11:30 A.M.–3:30 P.M.), with three sittings for dinner (5, 6:45, and 8:45 P.M.). Cocktails in Tap Room. AE, MC, V.

Christiana Campbell's Tavern. *Expensive.* Waller St., opposite the Capitol at eastern end of the Historic Area; 229–2141. Mrs. Campbell's original tavern (1771) was one of George Washington's favorite eating places. Brunch, served daily from 10 A.M. to 2:30 P.M., features pecan waffles, omelets, and skillet-fried chicken. Dinner — 5:30 till 9:30 P.M. — features seafood, Christiana Campbell's Special Dinner (chowder, fried chicken, ham, and trimmings), steak, and spoon bread. AE, MC, V.

Kings Arms Tavern. *Expensive.* Duke of Gloucester St., midway between Botetourt and Blair sts.; 229–2141. The third of these reconstructed taverns, the Kings Arms was Williamsburg's most genteel in the 18th century. Like its two sister taverns, the Kings Arms re-creates, through its food and furnishings, an atmosphere of gracious Colonial dining. The luncheon menu (11:30 A.M.–2:30 P.M.) features light fare,

THINGS TO SEE AND DO

The following pages contain a comprehensive checklist of major attractions in and around the Historic Triangle and elsewhere on the Virginia Peninsula. Although the greater number of these attractions are of historical interest, the editors recognize that even dedicated history buffs may want to step out of the Colonial period from time to time to sample some of the Peninsula's other attractions, especially if they are traveling with children. As in the two preceding chapters, the attractions below are grouped geographically, then listed alphabetically under various subheadings. These listings are meant to complement, not supplant, our earlier text, which presents the Story of America's Colonial Past, then guides you through the Experience. Each is essential to a full understanding of the beginning, middle, and end of the Colonial period — those years between the founding of Jamestown and the battle at Yorktown.

Jamestown

 COLONIAL NATIONAL HISTORICAL PARK (JAMESTOWN ISLAND). Located on the banks of the James River at the western end of Colonial Parkway, 23 miles from its Yorktown terminus. Access also from Rte. 31, Jamestown Rd. The Historical Park, site of the first permanent English settlement (1607), is adjacent to Festival Park (below). There is a parking lot and Visitor Center, with exhibits, and introductory film, and touring brochures. Walking tours, some conducted by Park Service rangers, and 3-mile or 5-mile loop drives through the island's woods and marshes begin here. Open daily 8:30 A.M.–4:30 P.M. and later from spring into the fall. Admission is $3 per car, 50 cents per bicycle.

 COLONIAL PARKWAY. An attraction in its own right, this 23-mile scenic drive links Jamestown with Williamsburg and Yorktown. Access at either end, Williamsburg, or Rte. 199, east and west of Williamsburg. There are no service stations along the parkway, which curves gently through wooded hills and skirts the James River to the west and York River to the east. Markers, overlooks, and picnic areas at Great Neck (south of Williamsburg) and Ringfield (midway between Williamsburg and Yorktown). Speed limit: 45 m.p.h.

CONFEDERATE FORTIFICATIONS. Earthen works from a later period (America's Civil War, 1861–1865) can still be seen on the island.

DALE HOUSE. Craftsmen re-create the style of pottery that was used by Jamestown colonists in the early 17th century. Objects on display are for sale.

FESTIVAL PARK. Adjacent to Colonial National Historical Park (slightly upriver), with access from Colonial Parkway, Rte. 31, or the Scotland Ferry across the James River. Jamestown Festival Park is a re-creation of America's first permanent English settlement. Tours

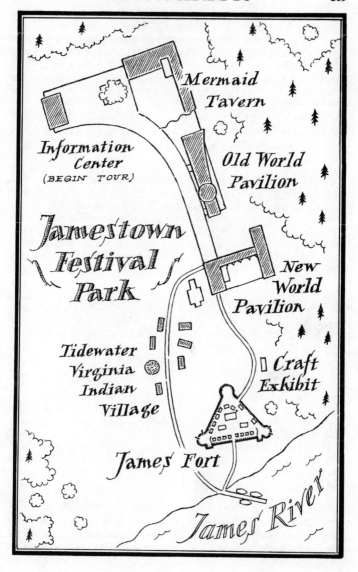

begin at the Information Center and include the Old and New World Pavilions, re-creations of a Tidewater Virginia Indian Village and James Fort, and (at a river pier near the Scotland Ferry slip) full-scale replicas of the settlers' three ships — *Susan Constant, Discovery,* and *Godspeed.* There is a craft exhibit area near the fort. Opened in 1957, Festival Park has a gift shop and an indoor-outdoor restaurant, the Mermaid Tavern (see Places to Eat, above). Open daily, except Christmas and Jan. 1, 9 A.M.–5 P.M., and longer in July and August. Adults $4, children half price. Combination Jamestown-Yorktown tickets available. For information, call the Foundation, 229–1607 (see also *Facts at Your Fingertips* section).

FIRST LANDING SITE. It is believed the first English settlers landed at a spot that now lies approximately 125 feet offshore, a short distance upriver from the Old Church. The shoreline has eroded in the past three or so centuries, and there is now a seawall to protect the bank. The first small English fort probably stood near here. (The settlers had landed earlier [Apr. 26] on Cape Henry, and again at present-day Hampton, before the Jamestown landing in mid-May 1607.)

FIRST STATEHOUSE. Brick work that is probably the foundation of the first Virginia Statehouse has been uncovered near the banks of the James River. Jamestown was the first capital of Virginia for 92 years.

GLASSHOUSE. Costumed craftsmen demonstrate the art of glassblowing as it was practiced by the colonists after 1608.

MEMORIAL CHURCH. Adjacent to Old Church Tower and built in 1907 on the foundations of the colony's original church, some of which can still be seen. There is a Colonial cemetery beside the church and the tower.

"NEW TOWNE." Well-marked foundations and original streets of Jamestown after the settlement expanded about 1620. Identifiable dwellings are labeled, some with diagrams. A stroll through the streets and lanes of this 17th-century "cittie" is a pleasant journey back in time.

OLD CHURCH TOWER. The only high-standing ruin in Jamestown, the Old Church Tower is a ghostly reminder of the original (1639) brick church. The tower is near the river, and now a part of Memorial Church (see above).

SETTLEMENT CELEBRATION. An annual event held on May 12 to commemorate the arrival of the first English settlers in 1607. Special tours and activities. There are Easter sunrise services each year at Memorial Church and the Old Church Tower (see above). Open to the public.

WILLIAMSBURG SCOTTISH FESTIVAL. Jamestown Festival Park. Piping, drumming, and Highland dancing in Sept. Scottish vendors and a pub tent, plus activities for children. Contact Williamsburg Scottish Festival, Box 866, Williamsburg 23187 for information.

Colonial Williamsburg

BUSES — HISTORIC AREA. Colonial Williamsburg's touring buses make a complete circuit of the Historic Area, making 10 scheduled stops, including the Visitor Center (see below), adjacent to the northern boundary of the restored or reconstructed 18th-century Colonial town. The bus route and stops are shown on the two-page map of the Historic Area. Visitors may board or disembark at any scheduled stop along the route. Although the Basic Ticket will admit you to most exhibits, a separate ticket or Patriot's Pass is required for the DeWitt Wallace Decorative Arts Gallery, Governor's Palace, Abby Aldrich Rockefeller Folk Arts Center (all below), or Carter's Grove Plantation, which is 7 miles from Colonial Williamsburg (see In and Around Williamsburg). Tickets may be purchased at the Visitor Center or the Information Station at Bus Stop 8 (see below). The Historic Area is closed to private motor vehicles from 8 A.M. until 6 P.M., and later during special events or the peak summer touring season.

Bus Stop 1. The first stop after the Visitor Center, Bus Stop 1 is opposite Robertson's Windmill on N. England St., a few steps from the Governor's Palace and Gardens, the Coach House (Wheelwright), and Brush-Everard House on the east side of Palace Green.

Bus Stop 2. Market Square near the corner of Nicholson and Queen sts., opposite Peyton Randolph House. Geddy Foundry, Geddy House and Shop, Courthouse of 1770, Magazine and Guardhouse, and Chowning's Tavern (see Places to Eat) are all a short stroll from here.

Bus Stop 3. Corner of Nicholson and Botetourt sts., a short block east of the Musical Instrument Maker and Cabinetmaker, at the intersection of Nicholson and Colonial sts.

Bus Stop 4. Waller St., midway between Nicholson and Francis sts., at the east or "downtown" end of the Historic Area. Opposite Christiana Campbell's Tavern (see Places to Eat), just east of the Capitol, and near the Public Gaol, this stop is a short walk from Benjamin Powell House on Waller St. or the Gunsmith, south of the Capitol on Francis St.

Bus Stop 5. Across from the Williamsburg Inn oval (see Places to Stay and Places to Eat).

Bus Stop 6. Parking lot off S. England St., opposite the Craft House and near the Abby Aldrich Rockefeller Folk Arts Center.

Bus Stop 7. S. England St., at Williamsburg Lodge and Conference Center (see Places to Stay and Places to Eat). Also near the Folk Arts Center and the Clubhouse (see Places to Eat), and opposite the Golden Horseshoe and Spotswood Golf Courses.

Bus Stop 7A. S. Henry St. on the west end of the Historic Area, at the Public Hospital and near DeWitt Wallace Decorative Arts Gallery.

Bus Stop 8. S. Henry St. near the corner of Duke of Gloucester St., "uptown" in Colonial Williamsburg. This next to the last scheduled stop inside the Historic Area is at the Information Station, opposite Merchants Square and a short block from the College of William and Mary at the intersection of Boundary St. and Richmond and Jamestown rds.

Bus Stop 9. N. England St. at the Public Footpath to the Visitor Center. This is the last stop for those who may prefer not to ride back to the Visitor Center proper. The Public Footpath comes out close to the South Parking Lot.

BRUSH-EVERARD HOUSE East side of Palace St., near the Governor's Palace. Restored home of a wealthy civic leader, Thomas Everard (1755–1781) and built by John Brush, gunsmith, armorer, and first Keeper of the Magazine on Market Square, the original structure was completed in 1717. The 300-volume library was assembled from a list compiled by Thomas Jefferson for a well-to-do planter of average intellectual interests. Ticket required.

BRUTON PARISH CHURCH. Corner of Duke of Gloucester and Palace sts. This Episcopal church has been in continuous use since 1715. The walls, windows, and west gallery are part of the original structure. It is said that the stone baptismal font was brought to Williamsburg from an earlier church at Jamestown. Bruton Parish Church was the most important building at Middle Plantation, where the parish was established in 1674. Admission by donation.

THE CAPITOL. Foot of Duke of Gloucester St., east end of Historic Area. Home of the House of Burgesses and the Council, the two houses of the legislature in Colonial Virginia, the Capitol, an imposing H-shaped building, rebuilt on its original foundations, was the scene of Patrick Henry's fiery "Caesar-Brutus" speech in 1765, the Resolution for Independence in 1776, and Thomas Jefferson's Statute for Religious Freedom. Ticket required.

COLLEGE OF WILLIAM AND MARY. "Uptown" Colonial Williamsburg, intersection of N. and S. Boundary sts., Duke of Gloucester St., and Richmond and Jamestown rds. Chartered in 1693 and named for King William and Queen Mary of England, the college was one of two important institutions that transformed Williamsburg from a village of a tavern, a few stores, and several houses along a winding path into a thriving Colonial urban center. (The other was Bruton Parish Church, established at Middle Plantation in 1674.) Noteworthy at the college are the Wren Building (1695–1732), President's House (1732–1733), and The Brafferton (1723), original structures that complement each other as fine examples of 18th-century architecture. The Wren Building was the first major Williamsburg structure to be restored. Ticket not required.

COURTHOUSE OF 1770. An original landmark building, the Courthouse of 1770 fronts on Duke of Gloucester St. and dominates Market Square. Information, general admission tickets, and tickets for special tours and events can be obtained here. All tours leave from the Courthouse.

 DE WITT WALLACE DECORATIVE ARTS GALLERY. Between S. Henry and Nassau sts., west corner of Historic Area, and entered through lower lobby of Public Hospital. An outstanding collection of English and American decorative arts from the 17th century to the early 19th century. Special lectures, musical events, and craft programs. Gift shop, cafe for luncheon and tea, and bookstore. Admission ticket or Patriot's Pass.

DUKE OF GLOUCESTER STREET. "Main Street" in Colonial Williamsburg — the college to the Capitol. Lined on both sides with houses, taverns, and shops, there is a cooper (Taliaferro-Cole Shop) near the corner of Nassau; a bootmaker across from the lower end of Palace St.; a printer-binder at the Post Office, between Colonial and Botetourt sts.; an archaeological exhibit, blacksmith shop (James Anderson House), and a music teacher's room on the south side of the street, between Colonial and Botetourt sts.; a milliner (Margaret Hunter Shop) just east of Botetourt, and Pasteur & Galt Apothecary Shop, a bit further along toward the Capitol. Tickets required at the above exhibit.

EATING PLACES (HISTORIC AREA). Chowning's Tavern, Duke of Gloucester and Queen sts.; Christiana Campbell's Tavern, Waller St., near York; and King's Arms Tavern, Duke of Gloucester St. (see Places to Eat, preceding chapter). Dining in a Colonial atmosphere.

FOLK ART CENTER (ABBY ALDRICH ROCKEFELLER). Located between Williamsburg Inn and Lodge, just off S. England St. American folk art in oil, watercolor, ink, and needlepoint. This outstanding collection was donated to Colonial Williamsburg by Mrs. Rockefeller and is housed in a museum that was built in her memory by her husband, John D. Rockefeller, Jr. Ticket required.

GEDDY FOUNDRY AND WORKSHOP. Corner of Palace and Duke of Gloucester sts. The restored James Geddy House, Workshop, and Foundry was the home and workplace of leading 18th-century gunsmiths, cutlers, jewelers, and engravers. Ticket for home and Foundry, but not for the Silversmith Shop, where silver, gold, pewter, bronze, and brass reproductions are sold.

GOVERNOR'S PALACE. Northwest Historic Area, facing Palace St. and Palace Green. The imposing residence of seven royal governors and the first two governors of the Commonwealth of Virginia — Patrick Henry and Thomas Jefferson. Completed in 1722, the palace has been reconstructed on its original foundations and completely refurbished. Within the palace walls are a stable, kitchen, and the gardens. Separate ticket or Patriot's Pass for the palace, but not for the gardens or Coach House, where the Wheelwright demonstrates his craft in the stable area. Ticket may be obtained at Robert Carter North Quarters at the north end of Palace St., near the entrance to the palace.

GUNSMITH (AYSCOUGH HOUSE). North side of Francis St., between Blair and Waller sts. Originally purchased as a tavern in 1768 by Christopher and Anne Ayscough. This small frame structure houses

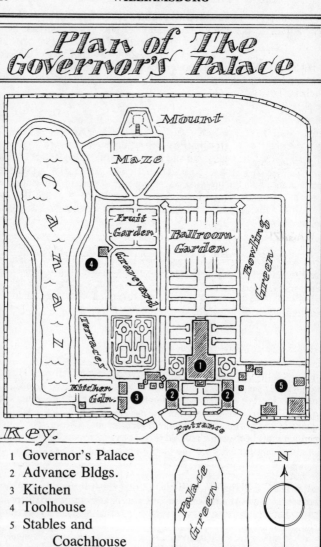

Plan of The Governor's Palace

Mount

Maze

Canal

Fruit Garden

Ballroom Garden

Bowling Green

Graveyard

Terraces

Kitchen Gdn.

Entrance

Palace Green

Key.
1 Governor's Palace
2 Advance Bldgs.
3 Kitchen
4 Toolhouse
5 Stables and
   Coachhouse

N

a gunsmith, who produces exact replicas of fowling pieces, rifles, and pistols that were used by Colonial Virginians. Ticket required.

HARNESSMAKER. Elkanah Deane Shop and Forge, George St., between Nassau and Palace sts. Leatherworking, from saddles to water buckets. Ticket required.

INFORMATION STATION. Located at Bus Stop 8, corner of Duke of Gloucester and S. Henry sts., west end of Historic Area and across from Merchants Square. Tickets, rest rooms, and information available.

MAGAZINE AND GUARDHOUSE. Market Square, between Duke of Gloucester and Francis sts. The red brick, octagonal Magazine, an original building, served as arsenal for the Virginia colony. Authentic firearms and other military equipment are exhibited here, and visitors can see uniformed militiamen marching, shooting muskets, or firing a cannon. A 1750 fire engine is housed at the nearby Guardhouse. Ticket required.

MARKET SQUARE. Bordered on the north by Nicholson St., on the south by Francis St., and bisected east and west by Duke of Gloucester St. In this green open area, midway between the college and the Capitol, see the Courthouse of 1770, the Magazine and Guardhouse, St. George Tucker House, Peyton Randolph House, and Market Square Tavern. Chowning's Tavern (see Places to Eat) is on Market Square at the corner of Duke of Gloucester and Queen sts. A lively open-air market during the Colonial period, Market Square was also the mustering grounds for the local militia.

MARKET SQUARE TAVERN. Corner of Duke of Gloucester and Queen sts., opposite Chowning's Tavern. A hostelry for more than 200 years; Thomas Jefferson was its most celebrated lodger. A restored original building.

MUSICAL INSTRUMENT MAKER AND HAY'S CABINETMAKING SHOP. North side of Nicholson St., at head of Colonial St. Two operating craft shops share this reconstructed building. In the larger cabinet shop, fine furniture is produced with hand tools and foot-powered lathes from favorite 18th–century woods — Virginia cherry and walnut, and imported mahogany. Next door, the maker of musical instruments produces violins, harpsichords, and English guitars. Ticket required.

PEYTON RANDOLPH HOUSE. Corner of N. England and Nicholson sts., across from Market Square. A restored white frame, three-part house, the first section built about 1715. The Randolphs were the first family of Williamsburg during the Colonial period, and the house was a center for numerous social and political gatherings. It is furnished with English and American antiques. Ticket required.

BENJAMIN POWELL HOUSE. Waller St., near Nicholson St. Also known as the Powell-Waller House and Office, these restored buildings were named for Benjamin Powell, who acquired the property in 1763. Ticket required.

THE PUBLIC GAOL. Nicholson St., north of the Capitol. Although the Public Gaol (pronounced "jail") was described in the 18th century as a "strong sweet prison," it is today a grim reminder of crime and punishment in Colonial Virginia. Its prisoners included criminals, pirates, debtors, and lunatics, plus "Hair Buyer" Hamilton, the British governor of the Northwest Territory, who was accused of paying Indians for American scalps. Ticket required.

PUBLIC HOSPITAL. Between S. Henry and Nassau sts., at the southwest corner of the Historic Area. The first public institution in British North America (1773) devoted exclusively to treating the mentally ill. Destroyed by fire in 1885 and completely rebuilt. Ticket required.

RECREATION. Lawn bowling, croquet, swimming, and tennis at Williamsburg Inn, and two golf courses — the 18-hole championship Golden Horseshoe and the 9-hole Spotswood Course — opposite Williamsburg Lodge and adjacent to the inn.

REFRESHMENTS. North side of Nicholson St., near Queen St.; Corner of Nicholson and Botetourt sts.; off Waller St., behind the Capitol Building; the corner of Botetourt and Francis sts.; Market Square at Francis and Queen sts.; north side of Duke of Gloucester St., near the Courthouse of 1770; and the north end of Palace St., at Robert Carter Office.

REST ROOMS. Off Waller St., immediately east of the Capitol Building; Bassett Hall, south of Francis St.; Francis St., near corner of Queen St., on southeast corner of Market Square; Information and Ticket Station, corner of S. Henry and Duke of Gloucester sts.; Governor's Palace, north of Palace Green; and opposite the Wheelwright, between Palace and N. England sts.

ROBERTSON'S WINDMILL. N. England St., across from Bus Stop 1. A reconstructed wind-driven windmill for grinding grain, built in 1732 on land owned by one of Williamsburg's leading citizens, William Robertson. Ticket required.

SHOPPING (HISTORIC AREA). Craft House, near Williamsburg Inn, official display and sales center for Williamsburg reproductions, gifts, and souvenirs; **Tarpley's, Prentis,** and **Greenhow** — general stores on Duke of Gloucester St.; **Geddy Shop** and the **Golden Ball,** jewelry and silver on Duke of Gloucester St.; the **Colonial Post Office,** featuring maps and prints, and the **Grocer's Shop,** both on Duke of Gloucester St.; **McKenzie's Apothecary,** offering herbs, spices, and candles, on Palace St., and the **Bake Shop,** behind Raleigh Tavern, north side of Duke of Gloucester St., between Botetourt St. and the Capitol. There is a large bookshop, featuring Colonial Williamsburg publications at the Visitor Center.

ST. GEORGE TUCKER HOUSE. Nicholson St., between Palace and N. England sts. One of the most admired private residences in Colonial Williamsburg, owned by the same family since 1788.

TOURS AND CARRIAGE RIDE. Tricorn Hat Tour, 2 ½-hour guided tour, ages 7–11, daily mid-June to late August, and Easter and Christmas seasons; **Once-Upon-A-Town Tour,** ages 4–6, daily mid-June to late August; **Townsteader Program,** crafts for ages 8–14, daily June and July; **Lanthorn Tour,** guided craftshop tours at night; **The Escorted Tour,** 2-hour guided tour through Historic Area; and **Carriage Rides** through the area with costumed drivers. Contact Information Center or Station for details, times, and prices. Phone 229–1000.

WETHERBURN'S TAVERN. Duke of Gloucester St., near southeast corner of Botetourt St. A popular hostelry in the 18th century, this charming white tavern has been restored to pre-Revolutionary appearance. Furnished with the aid of an inventory from the estate of Henry Wetherburn, innkeeper from 1743 to 1760. Ticket required.

WYTHE HOUSE. Facing Palace Green, between George and Duke of Gloucester sts. Originally owned by George Wythe, teacher, jurist, and legislator, the Wythe House was George Washington's headquarters just before the siege of Yorktown. Ticket required.

In and Around Williamsburg

BASSETT HALL. Southeast corner of Historic Areas, with access from Francis and York sts. A restored 18th–century white frame house (circa 1760) on 585 acres of rolling woodland that was the Williamsburg home of Mr. and Mrs. John D. Rockefeller, Jr. On display are 125 pieces of American folk art. Open daily at 10 A.M., April through December. Reservations and special ticket required. Phone 229–1000.

BERKELEY PLANTATION. Rte. 5, west of Charles City, midway between Williamsburg and Richmond. Site of first official Thanksgiving in 1619. A beautifully furnished and restored James River mansion, built in 1726. Open daily, 8 A.M.–5 P.M.; restaurant 11 A.M.–4 P.M. Terraced boxwood gardens. Phone 795–2453.

 BUSCH GARDENS. U.S. 60E, 3 miles east of Williamsburg. The theme of this 360-acre family entertainment park is "The Old Country," featuring re-created English, Scottish, French, Italian, and German villages, plus rides, shows, live entertainment, shops, restaurants, and a monorail that whisks visitors to the Anheuser-Busch Hospitality Center and Tour. The Loch Ness Monster is one of the more sensational rides, but there are also a sedate Rhineland "cruise" and "Grimm's Hollow" rides for children. Open daily mid-May through Labor Day and on weekends only from early April through October. The Hospitality Center is open Mar. 19–Dec. 2. For the current Busch Gardens schedule or for further information, call 253–3350 or write to Sales Manager, The Old Country, Drawer FC, Williamsburg 23187.

CARTER'S GROVE PLANTATION. Banks of James River, 6 miles southeast of Williamsburg via Carter's Grove Country Road (one-way only) or from U.S. 60E, south of Busch Gardens. Completed in 1755, this handsome Georgian mansion stands on beautifully landscaped grounds. The site of a 17th-century settlement, Wolstenholme Towne, which was destroyed during an Indian uprising in 1622, lies below the river bluff. The site can be toured, weather permitting. Carter's Grove, which has a Visitor Reception Center, is open daily, March through November, and during the Christmas season. Phone 229–6883. Special ticket required.

EVELYNTON. Rte. 5, between Sherwood Forest and Plantation and Westover. Originally part of Westover Plantation, the original house was plundered during the Civil War Peninsula Campaign of 1862. The present mansion, a fair example of the Georgian Revival style, was built on the earlier foundations. Open daily 9 A.M.–5 P.M.

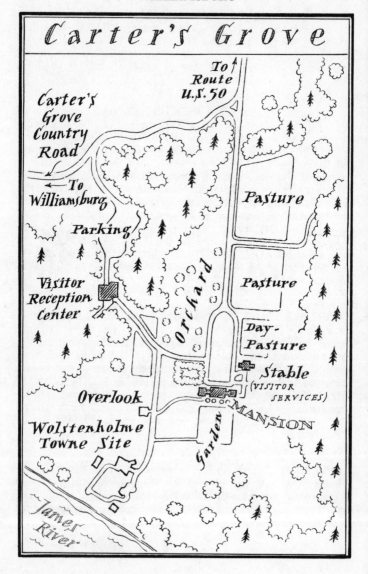

Carter's Grove

To Route U.S. 50

Carter's Grove Country Road

To Williamsburg

Parking

Pasture

Orchard

Pasture

Visitor Reception Center

Day-Pasture

Stable (VISITOR SERVICES)

Overlook

MANSION

Wolstenholme Towne Site

Garden

James River

MERCHANTS SQUARE. A pleasant, shaded shopping area between the College of William and Mary and Colonial Williamsburg, bisected east-west by Duke of Gloucester St. More than 50 shops and services, from ice cream and handcrafted sweets to pewter, old prints, and antique furniture. Places to eat include Berret's seafood restaurant and raw bar, Boundary and Francis sts.; and A Good Place To Eat and The Trellis, a restaurant and a cafe, both on Duke of Gloucester St. Shops include Alley Antiques, The Book House, and The Bookpress, Ltd., all on Prince George St.; The Golden Touch, a jeweler, also on Prince George St.; Master Craftsmen Shop, near Boundary St.; Prince George Graphics, prints and framing, Prince George St.; Scotland House, Ltd., tartan gifts, Duke of Gloucester St.; Sign of the Rooster, folk art and furniture, Henry St.; Shirley Pewter Shop, and the Scribner Book Store, both on Duke of Gloucester St.

SHERWOOD FOREST PLANTATION. Rte. 5 (John Tyler Highway), 18 miles west of Williamsburg; 829–5377. James River plantation home of John Tyler, 10th U.S. president. Also owned by William Henry Harrison, 9th president. Sherwood Forest is the longest frame house in America. Grounds open daily 9 A.M.–5 P.M. Corporate dinners in mansion by reservation.

SHIRLEY PLANTATION. 35 miles west of Williamsburg, slightly upriver from the Benjamin Harrison Bridge. First settled in 1613, Shirley Plantation mansion has a Queen Anne forecourt, which is unique in American architecture. Shirley was the home of Anne Hill Carter, mother of General Robert E. Lee, and has been owned by the Carter family since 1723. Open daily 9 A.M.–5 P.M.

SHOPPING — CRAFT HOUSES. Approved Williamsburg reproductions are available at two locations close to the Historic Area: off S. England St., adjacent to Williamsburg Inn, and the corner of Henry and Duke of Gloucester sts. in Merchants Square.

SHOPPING — GIFT SHOPS. DeWitt Wallace Decorative Arts Gallery, Bus Stop 7A, S. Henry St.; Carter's Grove (above), and in the lobbies of Williamsburg Inn and Williamsburg Lodge (see Places to Stay) or at the Motor House Cafeteria or Cascades Restaurant at the Visitor Center (see below).

SHOPPING — MERCHANTS SQUARE. (See Merchants Square, above.)

SHOPPING — OUTLETS AND MALLS. Some of the shopping meccas near the Historic Triangle are tourist attractions in their own right. None of them is more than a short drive from Williamsburg. Especially noteworthy are the following:

• **The Candle Factory.** (Williamsburg Soap and Candle Company), 7 miles west of Williamsburg, U.S. 60W at Rte. 607; 564–3354. Soap and candlemaking and exhibition, factory outlet, discount Emporium, shops, Country Store, and Smokehouse Restaurant. Open daily, except Thanksgiving, Christmas, and New Year's Day.

• **Outlets Ltd. Mall.** 6401 Richmond Rd. (U.S. 60W near Rte. 646), 5 miles northwest of Williamsburg. Discounted name brands in 30 stores. Terrace Cafe at the Mall.

• **Village Shops at Kingsmill.** U.S. 60E, between Rte. 199 and Busch Gardens; 229–5303. More than 40 shops and restaurants in a compact "village." Gifts, clothing, jewelry, home furnishings, and specialty foods in tasteful pleasant surroundings. Ample parking.

• **Williamsburg Pottery Factory.** 5 miles northwest of Williamsburg (in Lightfoot), just beyond Rte. 646; 564–3326. 18th-century salt-glaze pottery reproductions, china, glassware, and much more in 30 outlets on 130 acres. A sprawling factory outlet with hundreds of working craftsmen, plus imports from around the world. TopDog Restaurant. Open daily, except Christmas.

VIRGINIA SHAKESPEARE FESTIVAL. Phi Beta Kappa Theatre, College of William and Mary, Jamestown Rd., four blocks from Historic Area. Summer season (July–August). Elaborately staged professional Shakespearean productions. Single tickets, $7.50–$10.50; series tickets, $20–$26. Phone 253–4469 for schedule and tickets.

VISITOR CENTER (COLONIAL WILLIAMS-BURG). Located immediately adjacent to the Historic Area (east side), on Rte. 132Y, between Rte. 132 and Colonial Parkway. Access also from U.S. 60. A sprawling complex that includes the Visitor Center, cafeteria, Motor House, Cascades lodging and restaurant, group arrivals building, service station, and West (Green) and East (Blue) parking, with South (Red) parking directly across Rte. 132Y. Footpath and frequent buses to Historic Area. Information on accommodations, dining, exhibits, and activities. Tickets, reservations, and a continuous daily film, *Williamsburg — The Story of a Patriot.* (See **Buses — Historic Area,** under Colonial Williamsburg for scheduled stops.)

WATER COUNTRY USA. 3 miles east of Williamsburg, Rte. 199E, Exit 57B, I–64. Family fun for children and adults, this 25-acre park features flumes, slides, rapids, and surf. Restaurant. All-day admission tickets. For information, call 229–9300 or write Brochure Information, Water Country USA, Box 3088, Williamsburg 23187.

WESTOVER PLANTATION. Rte. 5, on the James River, between Berkeley and Sherwood Forest Plantations. Considered the nation's premier example of Georgian architecture, Westover's Colonial mansion is complemented by 150-year-old trees and a great lawn that sweeps down to the river. Grounds, historic outbuildings, and garden open year round. Adults, $2; children, 50 cents. Mansion open five days during Historic Garden Week.

WOLSTENHOLME TOWNE SITE. (See Carter's Grove, above.)

YORK RIVER STATE PARK. I–64 Croaker Exit, 8 miles northwest of Williamsburg, then a mile north on Rte. 607 to Rte. 606E. A natural preserve of woodlands and marshes covering 2,491 acres. Picnicking, water recreation, and nature trails. Some fees. Open daily. Call 564–9057 for further information.

Yorktown

COLONIAL NATIONAL HISTORICAL PARK (YORKTOWN BATTLEFIELD). Located on the bluffs above the York River at the eastern end of Colonial Parkway, about 13 miles from Colonial Williamsburg and 23 miles from Jamestown. Access from Colonial Parkway, Rte. 238 (Williamsburg Rd.), or U.S. 17, which spans the York River from Yorktown to Gloucester Point. Battlefield and Encampment tours begin at the National Park Service Visitor Center (extreme eastern terminus of the Parkway), but those touring the *total* area are advised to first visit the Yorktown Victory Center (see the last listing below). There are walking tours and 7-mile and 9-mile loop drives of the Battlefield and Encampment area, respectively. The *Visitor* Center, not to be confused with the Yorktown *Victory* Center, features Revolutionary War artifacts and exhibits, and an outdoor terrace overlooking the Battlefield. Open daily, except Christmas. Phone 898-3400.

MONUMENT TO ALLIANCE AND VICTORY. Foot of Main St., Yorktown, on a grassy plot between Zweibrucken Rd., Comte de Grasse St. (honoring the French admiral who blockaded the British fleet), and the York River. A 95-foot granite tower that commemorates the American-French alliance during the Revolutionary War.

THE MOORE HOUSE. Point **E** on the Yorktown Battlefield Tour (below), Moore Lane at the end of Moore House Rd. (Rte. 238, south of Yorktown). It really ended here — first a siege, then a war — in this modest 18th-century frame house that looks out over a sloping green lawn toward the widening mouth of the river. A visit to Moore House is a moving experience, for it was in these small rooms that a strapping young nation dictated its stern surrender terms to its humbled and exhausted parent. Park service rangers conduct tours through the house, which has been refurnished in period furniture. Don't overlook the Moore House brochure, which tells the story of the house and the British surrender at Yorktown. It is also interesting to note that other ghostly soldiers have trod these floors, and Moore House again heard the rumble of heavy artillery during General McClellan's Peninsular Campaign in the early years of the Civil War. The house, which sat in

No-Man's-Land, between Confederate troops entrenched in Yorktown and Union Forces on nearby Wormley Creek, was severely damaged by shellfire and by soldiers foraging for fire wood. Some minor repairs were made in 1881 for the Centennial Celebration of the victory over Cornwallis, but the house again sat derelict until the early 1930s when it was fully restored by the Park Service. Moore House is open daily, mid-June through Labor Day, and then on weekends only through mid-October. Admission is free, but donations are accepted for the printing of the Moore House brochure.

NATIONAL CIVIL WAR CEMETERY. Near **Point B,** Yorktown Battlefield Tour. Located at the intersection of Union and Surrender rds., the Civil War Cemetery is a quiet reminder of a second time Americans fought and died in these now peaceful fields, this time against each other. Of the 2,183 Civil War soldiers buried here, the names of more than half are unknown.

NELSON HOUSE. Nelson and Main sts., Yorktown. A restored Georgian mansion built in the 1700s. Costumed actors re-create the life of Thomas Nelson, Jr., a signer of the Declaration of Independence. Note the siege cannonballs lodged in the side of the house. The house, which is open daily from mid-June through Labor Day, is part of Colonial National Historical Park. Admission fee. Phone 898–3400.

SHIPWRECK PROJECT. York River, end of Water St., a few blocks downriver from the Victory Center (below). Here, in one of the most ambitious archaeological projects in North America, the Virginia Research Center is excavating the hull of one of General Cornwallis' ships, which was sunk during the Siege of Yorktown. From a special pier, you can watch divers at work. Admission fee.

STROLLING THROUGH YORKTOWN. Yes, Virginia, there *is* a Yorktown. First settled in 1691, the old Towne of York still exists as a quiet little community on the banks of the York River. The town faces Gloucester Point on the opposite bank. The two points are linked by the George P. Coleman Memorial Bridge (north-south, U.S. 17). Yorktown is also accessible via Rte. 238, which curves in from the west and north to run parallel to the York River cliffs and merge

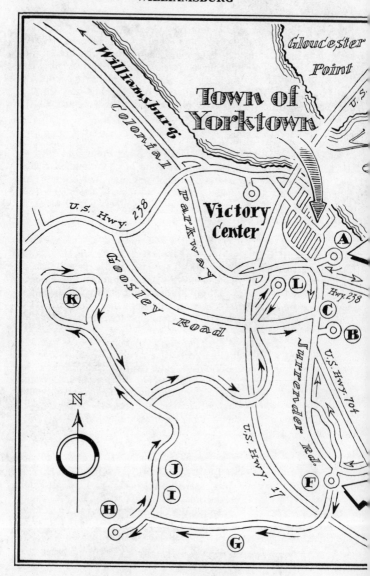

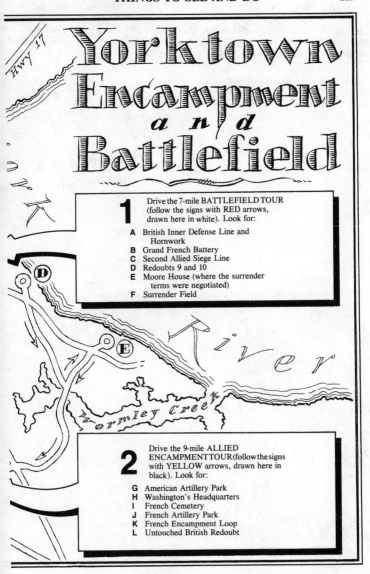

Yorktown Encampment *and* Battlefield

1 Drive the 7-mile BATTLEFIELD TOUR (follow the signs with RED arrows, drawn here in white). Look for:

A British Inner Defense Line and Hornwork
B Grand French Battery
C Second Allied Siege Line
D Redoubts 9 and 10
E Moore House (where the surrender terms were negotiated)
F Surrender Field

2 Drive the 9-mile ALLIED ENCAMPMENT TOUR (follow the signs with YELLOW arrows, drawn here in black). Look for:

G American Artillery Park
H Washington's Headquarters
I French Cemetery
J French Artillery Park
K French Encampment Loop
L Untouched British Redoubt

into Water St. at the bridge. Surrounded on the south and southwest by the Battlefield, Encampment Area, and Surrender Field, Yorktown is *what* it is because of what it *was* — a bustling little Colonial seaport, just off Chesapeake Bay, that in the fall of 1781 was the reluctant stage for General Lord Cornwallis' grand finale and the final curtain on England's Colonial America dream. Today a small riverside community, Yorktown is bounded on the north by Ambler St., with Zweibrucken Rd. less than a dozen streets to the south and Main St. running north-south through the middle of town. Yorktown lies between the Victory Center to the north and the Battlefield Visitor Center (see both below) to the south. The two sites, less than a mile apart, are the small trap that snapped shut and defeated a besieged British army. Note while strolling through town **Grace Episcopal Church** (1697) at the river end of Church St.; **Swan Tavern,** Main and Ballard sts., a reconstructed 18th-century tavern (now an antique shop) that blew up in 1863, and the 18th-century–style reconstructed **York County Courthouse,** Main St. opposite Swan Tavern. Courthouse records date from 1633. Open Monday through Friday, closed holidays.

SURRENDER FIELD (YORKTOWN BATTLEFIELD). Point F on

the Battlefield and Encampment Tours (see both below). Come here last — and stand, listen, and think. Come here, if you can, on a warm day in autumn, when the grass is browning, the back lanes are dusty, and the trees are beginning to turn red, yellow, and orange. Come on the kind of day it must have been on October 19, 1781, when a defeated British army marched out of Yorktown, past twin files of American and French soldiers, and laid down their arms on this quiet Tidewater meadow. Come in autumn, or in spring, summer, or winter, but visit this place at least once in your lifetime for an experience you will always remember. Surrender Field, which is maintained with tasteful dignity by the National Park Service, is open daily, except Christmas.

YORKTOWN ALLIED ENCAMPMENT TOUR.

A 9-mile drive, starting at the Visitor Center or at **Point F** on the map, between Surrender Field and U.S. 17. The editors believe that visitors will understand the siege better if they drive this tour first, follow it with the Battlefield Tour, and conclude with a solemn, even emotional, visit to Surrender Field (above). The Encampment Tour is a behind-the-scenes look at the buildup of American and French troops and artillery in the gullies and woods a mile or so south of the British defense lines around

Yorktown. Driving along this quiet and shaded road, it is easy to picture American and French soldiers moving guns, food, and ammunition forward to the combat troops on the line. Follow the YELLOW arrows to visit the American artillery park, Washington's headquarters, French cemetery, French artillery park, French encampment, and finally an untouched British redoubt, where you will then be inside the defenders' lines.

 YORKTOWN BATTLEFIELD TOUR. A 7-mile drive, starting at the Visitor Center, inside the British inner defense line immediately south of Yorktown. Stand on the outdoor terrace of the Visitor Center and view the field through British eyes — red-coated soldiers crouching behind earthen mounds and hornworks below on your right or the British redoubts (fortified outposts) out on your left flank, defensive anchors near the steep cliffs above the river. Further out, across the wide field, but less than a musketball shot away, are the heavy guns and blue-coated soldiers of the Allied siege line. At the Visitor Center, the National Park Service provides visitors with a detailed map and printed guide sheet for both tours (see Colonial National Historical Park, above). Follow the RED arrows for the Battlefield Tour, which ends at Surrender Field. Along the way you will visit:

A. British Inner Defense Line. (The present earthen works near the parking lot date to the Civil War.) General Lord Cornwallis had fortified Yorktown and Gloucester Point on the north bank of the river in August 1781. He pulled his 8,300 soldiers back to this inner defense line when General Washington, with 17,600 French and American troops, moved in to lay siege to the town in late September. General Washington had arrived in Williamsburg on September 14 to take command of Allied forces on the Virginia Peninsula. The British line extended almost a mile and a half around Yorktown. The hornwork on your left, as you approach the first intersection, extended out from the main defenses to guard the road to Hampton.

B. Grand French Battery. The largest gun emplacement on the first siege line, stretching from this point eastward to the York River. It was dug by Allied troops one night in early October. The batteries opened fire on October 9.

C. Second Allied Siege Line. Two days later, Allied soldiers edged closer to the battered British defenses and dug this second siege line. The line could not be extended to the river until Redoubts 9 and 10 on the British left flank had been captured at night by 800 soldiers, half French and half American.

D. Redoubts 9 and 10. These small earthen forts were taken in darkness on October 14 in fierce hand-to-hand fighting. French losses numbered 15 dead and 70 wounded at Redoubt 9, while nine Americans were killed and about 25 were wounded taking nearby Redoubt 10. The Americans then placed their largest artillery batteries between the two captured redoubts and extended the siege line to the river. On the morning of October 17, with no hope of escape or reinforcement, General Cornwallis sued for surrender.

 E. The Moore House. The final Articles of Capitulation were hammered out by officers from both sides on October 18 in the home of Augustine and Lucy Moore, about a mile east of the battlefield on the banks of the York River (for details, see **Moore House,** above).

F. Surrender Field. Here, on October 19, 1781, in this quiet field, the British army laid down its arms, ending the siege of Yorktown and marking the beginning of the end of Britain's efforts to hold onto her rebellious American colonies. The editors recommend that visitors make Surrender Field (see above) their final stop after touring both the Encampment area and the Battlefield. The RED arrow tour markers will then take you back to the Visitor Center, or, if you prefer, you can drive north via U.S. 17 to Yorktown or the Yorktown Victory Center. (Watch the signs and don't cross the bridge unless you want to visit Gloucester Point, where a small garrison of frustrated British soldiers watched the siege and the defeat of Cornwallis' main force on the Yorktown side of the river.)

YORKTOWN VICTORY CENTER. Rte. 238, one block from U.S. 17. (Rte. 238 also crosses Colonial Parkway less than a ½ mile northwest of the Victory Center.) Watch for the red, white, and blue flag symbols when approaching the center. Some visitors, especially those with children, find it useful to begin their tour of the Yorktown area at the Victory Center, where they'll see the gallery of the American Revolution, a dramatic film, *The Road to Yorktown,* and multimedia exhibits and displays that tell the story of America's War for Independence from Bunker Hill to General Washington's "golden opportunity" at Yorktown. Open daily 9 A.M.–5 P.M., except Christmas and New Year's Day. Special group rates and combination tickets to the Victory Center and Jamestown Festival Park are available. Admission fee. Contact Yorktown Victory Center, Box 1976, Yorktown 23690, or call 887–1776.

Hampton

Hampton claims to be the oldest English-settled community in the United States. (Jamestown is a park, not a town.) The settlement began in 1610 at a place called Kecoughtan with the building of two stockades as protection against the Kecoughtan Indians. In the late 18th century, Hamptonians were harassed by pirates until the notorious "Blackbeard" was killed by Captain Henry Maynard. Piracy came to an end here when Blackbeard's crew was jailed in Williamsburg. Hampton was shelled in the Revolution, burned by the British in the War of 1812, and burned again by its own citizens in 1861 to prevent occupation by the Union, with just five houses surviving the last conflagration. Commercial fishing and defense are now the major industries, but this old community on the shores of Chesapeake Bay at Hampton Roads is working hard to expand its tourist attractions, some of which are listed below.

AEROSPACE PARK. 413 W. Mercury Blvd., U.S. 258 off I–64; 727–6108 (also for Hampton area touring information). Far removed from the Colonial period, but an education nonetheless. Jet aircraft and missile exhibits. Open daily. Free admission. Closed on major holidays.

BLUE GAP FARM. 60 Pine Chapel Rd.; 727–6347 or 727–6161. Fifteen acres of indigenous wildlife and a barnyard zoo, old and new farm equipment and artifacts, and a picnic area and playground. Free admission. Open Wednesday through Sunday, except New Year's Day, Thanksgiving, and Christmas.

HISTORIC SITES. Big Bethel Battlefield, Big Bethel Rd., is the site of the first "irregular" battle of the Civil War on June 10, 1861; **Syms-Eaton Museum,** 418 W. Mercury Blvd., features exhibits of local history; **Casemate Museum** at **Fort Monroe,** on Chesapeake Bay, off U.S. 258, includes tours, exhibits, and the history of the Fort, which began as a stockade in 1609 and was last rebuilt in the early 1800s; **St. John's Church** and **Parish Museum,** Court St. and W. Queen's Way, displays a Bible that dates back to 1599, in a church that dates from 1728, in a parish that was founded in 1610; **Hampton University Museum,** east end of Queen St., Exit 5, I-64, displays an outstanding collection of Indian and African artifacts in a university founded in 1868; and **Hampton Monument,** on the grounds of the VA Medical Center, between Mill Creek and Hampton River, Exit 4, off I-64, marks the approximate first Peninsula landing site in 1607 of the first English colonists, who then moved further upstream to settle at the place now called Jamestown. Further information about these and other Hampton sites and events can be obtained from the Hampton Information Center, 413 W. Mercury Blvd., Hampton 23666; 727-6108.

KECOUGHTAN INDIAN VILLAGE. 418 W. Mercury Blvd., adjacent to Syms-Eaton Museum (see Historic Sites, above) and close to Aerospace Park and the Hampton Visitor Center; 727-6248. A reconstructed Indian village, with a museum and guided tours. Free admission. Closed on major holidays.

NASA VISITOR CENTER. Langley Research Center, Rte. 134, at Langley Air Force Base. Self-guided tours and films, with more than 40 exhibits, for an exploration of the Challenge of Flight, Kitty Hawk to the Space Shuttle. Open noon–4:30 P.M.; closed New Year's Day, Easter, Thanksgiving, and Christmas. Free admission. Free parking. For information, phone 865-2855. Note: There is an annual Air Show in the spring at Langley A.F.B. Call 764-2018 for date and details.

Newport News

Newport News, adjacent to Hampton, at the southeastern tip of the Virginia Peninsula, is one of three cities that make up the Port of Hampton Roads. The third is Norfolk. Settled in 1619, Newport News has the world's largest shipbuilding firm, the Newport News Shipbuilding Company, which employs 25,000 workers. Hampton Roads, one of the world's finest natural harbors, is 14 miles long and 40 feet deep. It is formed by the James, York, Elizabeth, and Nansemond rivers as they pass into the Chesapeake Bay. Like neighboring Hampton, this old community shares much of the history that today attracts millions of visitors to the Historic Triangle, further up the Peninsula. Proud of its heritage, Newport News has its own attractions, some of which are listed below.

ARMY TRANSPORTATION MUSEUM. Fort Eustis, northwest end of Newport News on the James River; access from U.S. 60 or I–64; 878–3603. Fort Eustis is headquarters of the U.S. Army Transportation Corps, hence this outstanding collection of equipment for moving personnel and supplies on land and sea, as well as in the air. There is a Civil War earthen fort on the grounds. An auto tour and a film are offered. Free admission. Open daily, except New Year's Day and Christmas.

EXHIBITS. Peninsula Fine Arts Center, Museum Drive, 598–8175, features free exhibits by Tidewater and Virginia craftsmen (daily except Monday and major holidays), while **Peninsula Nature and Science Center**, 524 J. Clyde Morris Blvd. (Deer Park) has exhibits on natural science, and includes an aquarium, nature trails, and an observatory. The center is open daily, except Thanksgiving, Christmas, and New Year's Day. Admission fee. For further details, call 599–8000.

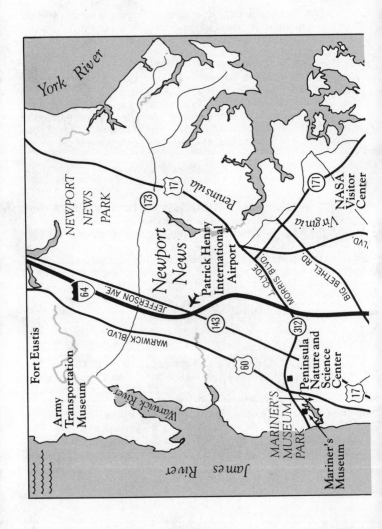

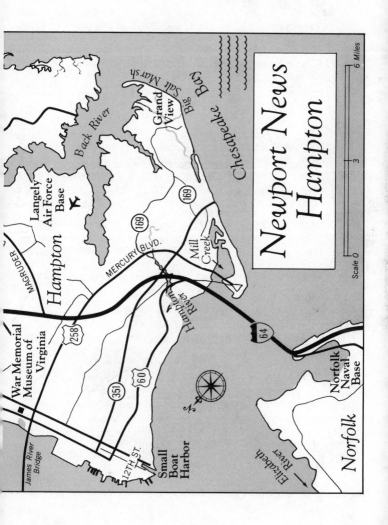

THE MARINERS' MUSEUM. 9285 Warwick Blvd., U.S. 60 (Exit 62-A off I–64); 595–0368. Located in a 550-acre natural Huntington Park, this nautical museum has been called "the best (of its kind) in the country." Conducted tours of 14 unique galleries tell the story of man at sea. Outstanding collections of ship models, figureheads, marine artifacts, and carvings. Featured are the August F. Crabtree Collection of Miniature Ships and a Sea Power Gallery. The 65,000-volume research library is open to the public. Open Monday through Saturday 9 A.M.–5 P.M., Sunday noon–5 P.M.; closed Christmas. Adults, $3; children 6–16, half price.

NEWPORT NEWS PARK. Located a mile north of the junction of rtes. 105 and 143, this 8,000-acre park has picnic areas, water recreation, nature trails, campsites, and three golf courses. Open all year. Some fees. For information, call 877–5381.

WAR MEMORIAL MUSEUM OF VIRGINIA. 9285 Warwick Blvd., with the Mariners' Museum (see above) in Huntington Park. More than 30,000 items — weapons, uniforms, art, and equipment — from the Revolution to Vietnam. Film collection and library. Open daily, except New Year's Day and Christmas. For information, call 247–8523.

WHARTON'S WHARF AND HARBOR CRUISES. 530 12th St., Small Boat Harbor, Newport News 23607; 245–1533. Two harbor cruises aboard the *Patriot* cruise vessel, featuring waterside views of Newport News Shipyard and the Norfolk Naval Base. One to four sailings daily, depending on the season and the weather, with the fullest schedule between mid-June and Labor Day. Also evening "harbor lights" cruises, June through August, and longer Intra-Coastal Waterway cruises, April through October. Prices range from $8 to $27.50 for adults, and $4 to $15 for children, depending on the type of cruise.

INDEX

(References to maps and plans appear in **boldface**.)